THINKERS OF THE EAST

IDRIES SHAH

THINKERS OF THE EAST

Studies in Experientialism

The rights that others have over you – remember them.
The rights that you have over others – forget them.
Sayedna Ali

THE OCTAGON PRESS
LONDON

Contents

Preface

ଉଉଉଉଉଉଉଉଉଉଉଉଉଉଉଉଉଉଉଉଉଉଉଉଉଉଉଉଉ

UNTIL, as it were, yesterday, it would have been impossible
to publish this book, in spite of the fact that the materials
which it contains have been an organic part of Eastern practical-
philosophy study for countless centuries. The reason is that the
highly articulate of both the East and West have generally
been in the grip of the belief that only a certain kind of organ-
ized thought can be used for learning. The fact is, however,
that all the precedents, all the books, all the traditions which
have produced the great thinkers of the past in the Orient
show almost no trace of what is today believed to be organiza-
tion.

If you were to ask a traditional Eastern sage for his 'system',
he would look at you as a modern physician would if you
asked for his 'panacea for all ills'. He might invite you to
apply to a seller of nostrums on a fairground. He would certainly diagnose you as a primitive who had still to learn the
first lesson about knowledge.

Any inspection of the 'specialist' literature on Eastern
thinkers and their schools will show the ludicrous situation
that the materials available have been more and more closely
examined, more and more carefully arranged, in an increasingly
mechanical form—not unaccompanied by puzzled mutterings
—and the products have become less and less. This fact has
been succinctly put by those who remark that scholars desire
to study mystics, but mystics never need to study scholars.

Fortunately, in places and in circles which have escaped the
modishness of a demand for over-simplification or rigid system
(where it has been realized that the essential need is to seek,
preserve and transmit knowledge), the manner of 'prescribing'
studies for individuals and groupings in accordance with teaching requirements alone has been continuously maintained.

With the current dying out of the least useful type of arid-minded pedants, who have succeeded only in giving scholasticism its undeservedly bad odour, the pendulum is swinging back.

This book contains, arranged in a manner commanded by the tradition and not by superficialist obsessional arranging, the materials belonging to the Sufi teaching, selected in accordance with the needs of the time. It might be termed applied specific experientialism.

The very widespread welcome of earlier volumes of similar material, from both academic and other circles, indicates that there is a taste for it, and perhaps a use.

IDRIES SHAH

Subjects Dealt With in
Thinkers of the East

SYSTEMS of study; the 'Sufi Secret'; problem-solving by non-linear thinking; methods of choosing disciples; special groupings for inner study; use and abuse of literature; different realms of thought; reasons for dismissing students; the role of higher teaching; various types of teachers; the 'Teacher of the Age'; clearing false assumptions; paradoxical behaviour; 'wonders and miracles'; special training; riches and poverty; acquiring objectivity; how people learn through 'parallel training'; testing would-be seekers; books and ceremonials; special invocatory formulae; the way to study the lives of former sages; reasons for so many different outward forms of teaching; distinguishing imitators from real instructors; comparisons between various dimensions of knowledge; observing basic motivations; teaching by demonstration; determining the common denominator in study; illustrations of the inward state; knowledge distinguished from opinion; self-observation; why analogies are employed; parable of the work of the people called The Designers; indirect learning system; means employed to convey 'equivalent thought'; examples of illustrative acting; effects of attending 'mystical ceremonies'; being 'useful in reality, not in appearance'; reasons for 'selling knowledge'; how disciples learn from specially constructed procedures; the effects of emotion and intellect on studies; astrological investigations; implanted suggestions; how higher thinkers affect events; instructional interchanges in mystical schools; making effective use of negative characteristics; the inner significance of outward service; alteration of expectancy; the creating of an air of mystery; the publication of nonsensical literature; materials projected in accordance with the possibilities of the

13

occasion; illustrating false impressions; anger; keeping methods and aims in alignment; courting criticism and reactions to it; worldly success and its value; methods and advantages in social activity; doctrine of premature 'payment' for effort; allegory of the human task; symbolism and effect in financial matters; legends of the spread of the Teaching; the reality of which 'man' is an allegory; the degree of capacity to perceive 'secret teachings'; learning by words and by signs; supercession of outward systems of teaching; the storing and transmitting of subtle communications; correcting incapacitating attitudes; disguised operations; the need to digest materials at a certain rate; allegory of the techniques of teachership; real and imagined desire.

A Death is Indicated

ᴛʜᴇʀᴇ was once a dervish who had sixty disciples. He had taught them as well as he could, and the time had come to undergo a new experience.

He called the disciples together and said:

'We must now go on a long journey. Something, I am not sure what, will happen on the way. Those of you who have absorbed enough to enter this stage will be able to accompany me.

'But first you must all memorize this phrase, "I must die instead of the dervish." Be prepared to shout this out at any time, whenever I raise both my arms.'

Some of the disciples started muttering among themselves, now highly suspicious of the dervish's motives. No less than fifty-nine of the sixty deserted him, saying, 'He knows that he will be in danger at some time, and is preparing to sacrifice us instead of himself!'

They said to him, 'You may even be planning some crime—perhaps even a murder; we can never follow you on terms like that.'

The dervish and his sole remaining companion started the journey.

Now a most terrible and unjust tyrant had seized the next city shortly before they entered it. He wanted to consolidate his rule with a dramatic act of force, and called his soldiery together.

He said to them:

'Capture some wayfarer of meek aspect and bring him for judgment in the public square. I propose to sentence him as a miscreant.'

The soldiers said, 'We hear and obey!' went into the streets and pounced upon the first travelling stranger they met. He happened to be the disciple of the dervish.

The dervish followed the soldiers to the place where the king sat, while all the citizenry, hearing the drums of death and already trembling with fear, collected around.

The disciple was thrown down in front of the throne, and the king said:

'I have resolved to make an example of a vagabond, to show the people that we will not tolerate unconformity or attempted escape. You are to die at once.'

At this the dervish called out in a loud voice:

'Accept *my* life, O Mighty Monarch, instead of the life of this useless youth! I am more blameworthy than he, for it was I who induced him to embark upon a life of wandering!'

At this point he raised both arms above his head, and the disciple cried out:

'Munificent King! Please allow me to die—I must die instead of the dervish!'

The king was quite amazed. He said to his counsellors:

'What kind of people are these, vying with one another to taste death? If this is heroism, will it not inflame the people against me? Advise me as to what to do.'

The counsellors conferred for a few moments. Then they said:

'Peacock of the Age! If this is heroism there is little that we can do about it, except to act more viciously until people lose heart. But we have nothing to lose if we ask this dervish why he is anxious to die.'

When he was asked, the dervish replied:

'Imperial Majesty! It has been foretold that a man will die this day in this place; and that he shall rise again and thereafter be immortal. Naturally, both I and my disciple want to be that man.'

The king thought, 'Why should I make others immortal, when I myself am not?'

After a moment's reflection, he gave orders that he should be executed immediately, instead of the wanderers. Then the worst of the king's evil accomplices, eager for immortality, killed themselves.

None of them rose again, and the dervish and his disciple went their way during the confusion.

Ordinary

RASHID SITARAZAD received a party of intending students whose heads were filled with his wonders and the excitement of arriving so near to the source of the Teaching.

He said:

'Let one of you be your spokesman, and let him tell me of your feelings.'

One of the visitors stepped forward and said:

'We are stimulated by the Presence, and eager for the Knowledge, and elevated by the Tradition.'

Rashid said:

'That is a truthful account of your feelings. Because you all love the exciting, I shall have to give you the banal. You are to learn through life. And life—the key to knowledge—is the most banal of all things. You will have to undergo experiences which will make you understand life, not make it more interesting.'

One of those present exclaimed:

'That man whom you asked to represent us speaks for himself, and yet we must all be judged by his behaviour!'

Rashid said:

'He may think that he speaks for all of you. You may think that he speaks only for himself. But it is I who have agreed that he speaks for all. Are you already disputing my authority? To do so shows that you crave excitement, and verifies the words which you are trying to refute!'

Bravery

A CERTAIN widely read and energetic man went to the Hakim Husseini, and said:

'I do not ask for myself, but I am sure that if you were me and met my friend Dilawar you would realize that he is nothing less than a Sufi, and that you would welcome him and make him a sharer in your investigations and a partner in your studies, and would revel in his delightful presence.'

The Hakim said:

'I do indeed admire your bravery (*dilawari*), for I have myself never been able to recognize a Sufi in such a manner as you have.

'Because my circle is proceeding on different assumptions, to welcome Dilawar might be a delight; but it would also mean dealing with him alone, for none of my companions is able to associate with such a man. The journey to adulthood begins with infancy, and if you have a class of infants and you know what their destination will be, this does not mean that you can take on a single extra student who in any case would need the association of an entire class of his contemporaries to enable him to make the requisite progress.'

A Disciple of Haidar

HAIDAR heard a disciple say:

'I am glad that I did not buy such-and-such a book, for now I have arrived at the Source of its knowledge I have saved myself pain and needless expense.'

After a year Haidar handed him a book, saying:

'You have served me for twelve months. The value of your labour has been a hundred dirhams. That is the cost of this book.

'You would not have paid a hundred silver pieces for such an inanimate object as a book, and few people would do so. But you have been made to pay for it, by me, and here it is.

'A camel is dear at a penny if you do not need a camel.

'A single word is cheap at a thousand gold pieces, if it is essential to you.

'If you wish to return to the Source of Being, you will always have to take the first step, even though you may be demanding to be allowed to take the hundredth step.'

The Most Great Name

A FAKIR in India asked a Sufi whether he would tell him the Most Great Name: the Hundredth Name of Allah. Those who know it can perform miracles, altering the course of life and of history. None may know it until he is worthy.

The Sufi said:

'In accordance with tradition, I must first give you the test which will show your capacity. You shall go to the gate of this city and remain there until nightfall, returning to me then to describe something which you will have witnessed.'

The fakir eagerly did as he was told. After nightfall he came back and gave his report to the sage in these terms:

'As instructed, I positioned myself at the city gate in a condition of alertness. The incident which most impressed me during the day concerned an old man. He wanted to enter our city with a huge load of firewood on his back.

'The gatekeeper insisted on his paying a tax on the value of his goods. The old man, being penniless, asked that he might be allowed to sell his wood first. Realizing that he was friendless and helpless, the gatekeeper forced him to hand over his wood, which he stole for himself. The old man was driven away with cruel blows.'

The Sufi said:

'What were your feelings when you saw this?'

The fakir answered:

'I desired even more strongly to know the Most Great Name. Had I known it, the case would have been different for that unfortunate and innocent wood-cutter.'

The Sufi said:

'O man born to attain felicity! I myself learned the Hundredth Name from my own Master, after he had tested my resolution and ascertained whether I was an impulsive

21

emotionalist or a servant of man, and after he had subjected me to experiences which would allow me to see my own thoughts and conduct.

'The Hundredth Name is for the service of all mankind, all the time. My Master was none other than the wood-cutter whom you saw today, by the city gate.'

The Book of Wisdom

SIMAB said:

'I shall sell the Book of Wisdom for a hundred gold pieces, and some people will say that it is cheap.'

Yunus Marmar said to him:

'And I shall give away the key to understanding it, and almost none shall take it, even free of charge.'

Kadudar and the Pilgrimage

A CERTAIN Kalandar on his travels fell in with the sage Kadudar, and asked him the question which had been puzzling him for many years:

'Why do you forbid your followers to make the pilgrimage? How can man forbid what has been commanded from On High?'

Kadudar, whose name means 'possessor of the gourd', held up a dried gourd and said:

'Can you forbid this pumpkin to be a pumpkin? Nobody can forbid the fulfilling of a celestial command; so that even if a man appeared to do so, in reality it would be impossible.

'The duty of the Guide, however, is to ensure that pilgrimages are not performed by people in an unsuitable inner state, just as the guardians of the Sanctuary will prevent anyone from carrying out the pilgrimage rites in an unsuitable outward state.

'All pilgrimage has an outward and an inward aspect. The ordinary man will help the pilgrim when he needs money or food, and will raise him up if he has collapsed on the road. The Man of the Path, minutely discerning similar necessities in the inner life, is compelled to give his aid in his own way.'

Dismissal

SOMEONE said to Bahaudin Naqshband:

'It must have caused you pain to dismiss a certain student.'
He said:

'The best of all ways to test and help a disciple, if it is possible, may be to dismiss him. If he then turns against you, he has a chance of observing his own shallowness and the defects which led to the dismissal. If he forgives you, he has an opportunity of seeing whether in that there is any sanctimoniousness. If he regains his balance, he will be able to benefit this matter of ours (the Teaching) and especially to benefit himself.'

Words of Israel of Bokhara

THE Teaching is like air.

Man dwells in it, but cannot realize by real feeling that but for it he would be dead.

He can see air only when it is polluted, as in smoke rising, and by its effects.

He sees polluted air, breathes it and imagines that it is a pure substance.

Deprived of it he dies. But when he is choking he has hallucinations, and hopes for remedies when what he needs is the restoration of air.

He may become aware of it, and profit more from it, by realizing that it is a common substance treated with such heedlessness that nobody observes its presence.

Lands of the Gurus

A CERTAIN merchant visiting a Sufi said to him:

'Some countries are absolutely full of gurus, spiritual teachers with formulas and doctrines of a certain kind. Why are there so few Sufi chiefs of local circles? Why is it that even these, when they are publicly known, turn out to be mere imitators or repeaters of exercises handed down by someone else?'

The Sufi said:

'These are two questions, but they have one and the same answer:

'India, for instance, is full of gurus and shrine-worshippers, and public Sufis of real truth are more than rare because the gurus and their followers are at play and the Sufis are at work. Without the Sufi work, humanity would die out. India is a land of snake-charmers; public gurus are man-charmers. They amuse the people. The secret saints work for the people. The activity of man is to seek the secret teachers. The activity of children is to seek amusement.

'Have you not observed the flocks of former disciples of gurus who daily surround us, and the fact that not one in a hundred can be admitted, for they have been taught to enjoy something which they should have been taught to learn instead?'

Nili

SOMEONE found out that Nili was giving his disciples exercises and music and entertainments, as well as encouraging them to read books and to meet in exotic places.

This critic said to the sage:

'I forget how many years it is that you have worked against such superficialities and fripperies! Now I discover that you are using them in your pretended teaching. Abandon this practice forthwith, or explain it to me.'

Nili said:

'I have neither to abandon nor to explain, but I am glad to tell you. This is the reason. I give exercises to people who can understand what they are for. Most people do not, and they are like people who have gone to the restaurant and fallen in love with the cook instead of eating the soup. People listen to music with the wrong ear, so I deny them music until they can benefit from it, not make play of it. Until they know what it is for, they consume music like people warming their hands at a fire which could be cooking something. As for environment, certain atmospheres are cultivated by aesthetes, who thus deprive themselves of their further value, and teach others to stop before they have gained anything of real worth. These are like people who have gone on a pilgrimage and can think only about the number of steps which they have taken.

'As to exercises, I cannot give them to anyone, any more than I can allow them to read books, until they learn that there is a deeper content than the shallowness which smells the aroma of the fruit and then forgets that it is there to be eaten. Nobody objects to the smelling, but all would soon be dead if they refused to eat.'

How Man is Sustained

IMAM PUTSIRR announced:

'People visit the Teacher of the Age to gain what are really small advantages.

'Did they but realize it, they should build upon the great advantages which they have always been given already by the Teacher of the Age.

'The greatest of these is that the whole human community, not just a flock of "believers", only continues to exist in physical form because of the work and the life of the Teacher of the Age.

'This is such an astonishing and unlikely fact that it is called, by the Elect, "the secret which is completely concealed by its immediate unlikelihood." '

Jan Fishan and the Seeker

A MAN came to Jan Fishan and said:

'I have followed many masters, and I am in contact with a great number of wise people. Please give me your own attention and help.'

Jan Fishan said:

'I can best help you by pointing out that you are being false to even one master, let alone "many", if you are still wandering about and applying to me, after you have found them. I can best serve you, if indeed you do know such masters, by beseeching you to return to one of them and really learning. If you had learnt anything, it would tell you not to run between two wells, like the thirsty and covetous dog which ultimately perished — not of thirst, but of exhaustion.'

Then Jan Fishan read the following passage from *Munaqib el-Arifin*:

Maulana Shamsudin Multi reports that Rumi said one day during a discourse that he loved Multi greatly, but that he had one fault. Multi begged to be told what it was. Rumi said it was to imagine that all kinds of things and people were of spiritual merit. He recited:

'Since many men have
The inwardness of Satan
— Should one hail
Everyone as a saint?
When your Inward Eye
Is opened —
The Real Master
Can then be perceived!'

When Multi's inner eye was opened, Rumi recited this verse and ordered all his disciples to commit it to memory:

'In this market-place of
Occult medicine-sellers:
Do not run hither and thither
From shop to shop.
But rather sit at the booth
Of the one who has the real remedy to give!'

Objectors

PEOPLE used to accuse Rumi of having strayed from the Right Path in allowing and encouraging plays, songs and music and other unusual activities.

He never answered these objections, according to *Munaqib el-Arifin*.

But other sources report him as saying:

'The accounts are always made up at the end of the day. Let us see, when a sufficient space of time has passed, whether it is our *work* which is remembered or the names of our critics.

'Everyone knows that there are lions and jackals. Although in modern times many jackals have induced people to believe that they are lions, the ancient rules always operate over the run of time.

'You have heard many stories which say, "There was once a lion ... " How many do you hear which begin, "There was once a jackal ... "?'

Exclusion

RAIS EL-AFLAK, 'The Lord of the Skies', who suddenly appeared in Afghanistan and then disappeared after giving a number of cryptic lectures, said:

'Almost all the men who come to see me have strange imaginings about man. The strangest of these is the belief that they can progress only by improvement. Those who will understand me are those who realize that man is just as much in need of stripping off rigid accretions to reveal the knowing essence, as he is of adding anything.

'Man thinks always in terms of inclusion into a plan of people, teachings and ideas. Those who are really the Wise know that the Teaching may be carried out also by exclusion of those things which make man blind and deaf.'

The Philosopher's Stone

IT is reported that Rumi, as a demonstration, endowed an ordinary stone with such characteristics that those who saw it thought that it was a ruby. Taken to a jeweller, it was sold for over a hundred thousand dirhams.

But, talking of transmutation, Rumi himself said:

'Using the stone of the philosopher to convert copper into gold is indeed wonderful.

'More wonderful still is the fact that, moment by moment, the philosopher's stone (man) is converted into copper—by his own heedlessness.'

Barbari and the Imitator

THE dervish Barbari, posing as a disciple, regularly attended the weekly meetings of an imitation Sufi who imagined that he was teaching the real Way.

Every time the dervish appeared at the meeting, he asked the supposed Sufi a ridiculous question.

After he had had to snap at him several hundred times, the pretender shouted at Barbari:

'You have been coming here for twelve years and all your absurd questions are only variations of the one which you have just asked!'

'Yes, I know,' said Barbari, 'but the delight which I get from seeing you so annoyed is my *only* vice.'

Iskandar of Balkh

His son asked Iskandar of Balkh on his deathbed:

'What is the source of your power, your wealth and your miracles?'

His father murmured:

'If I were to tell you, it would cut you off from contact with this source, so I cannot tell you where it is, only what it is.'

He continued:

'Our lifeline is the Sufi Way, and we are strangers as it were among savages on this earth, but now I go to join our own.'

His son said:

'Why did you not tell everyone this during your life? For this example of yours, which will live a thousand years, would cause men to enter the Sufi Way in throngs, and would give them the blessings of the Elect.'

Iskandar sighed and said:

'The greed to possess a secret would make most of them attracted, and the desire for more than others have got. My son, I taught abstemiousness all my life in the hope that it would still the covetousness which destroys man, even if he covets goodness.'

'Then what shall I do?' asked his son.

'You shall desire Truth for its own sake, and nothing for your own sake.'

'But how shall I know whether I am desiring something for myself and not for itself?'

'You shall become aware, through daily practice, that what you imagine to be yourself is concocted from beliefs put into you by others, and is not yourself at all. You shall seek the Teacher of the Age until you find him. And if you fail to recognize the Leader of the Epoch it will be because you inwardly reject him, not because he is not evident as what he is.'

This is the testimony of the great Sufi Suleiman Najami, the son of Iskandar of Balkh. Giving it to his own son, he said:

'In a long life, I cannot say that I have learned more than this, my father's bequest of wisdom to me. I do therefore offer it to you.'

Ali, Son of the Father of the Seeker

ᔧᔧᔧᔧᔧᔧᔧᔧᔧᔧᔧᔧᔧᔧᔧᔧᔧᔧᔧᔧᔧᔧᔧᔧᔧᔧᔧᔧᔧᔧᔧᔧ

ALI said:

'None may arrive at the Truth until he is able to think that the Path itself may be wrong.

'This is because those who can only believe that it must be right are not believers, but people who are incapable of thinking otherwise than they already think. Such people are not men at all. Like animals they must follow certain beliefs, and during this time they cannot learn. Because they cannot be called "humanity", they cannot arrive at the Truth.'

Rabia el-Adawiya

HASAN came upon Rabia one day when she was sitting among a number of contemplators, and said:

'I have the capacity of walking on water. Come, let us both go on to that water yonder, and sitting upon it carry out a spiritual discussion.'

Rabia said:

'If you wish to separate yourself from this august company, why do you not come with me, so that we may fly into the air, and sit there talking?'

Hasan said:

'I cannot do that, for the power which you mention is not one which I possess.'

Rabia said:

'Your power of remaining still in the water is one which is possessed by fish. My capacity, of flying in the air, can be done by a fly. These abilities are no part of real truth—they may become the foundation of self-esteem and competitiveness, not spirituality.'

Abboud of Omdurman

THEY asked Abboud of Omdurman:
   'Which is better, to be young or to be old?'
   He said:
   'To be old is to have less time before you and more mistakes behind. I leave you to decide whether this is better than the reverse.'

Ajami

HASAN asked Ajami:

'How did you reach your present heights of spiritual attainment?'

Ajami said:

'Through making the heart white in celestial contemplation, not by making paper black with writing.'

Conversion

MALIK, son of Dinar, relates this operation of behaviour and conversion:

Malik was exercised in mind about the debauched behaviour of a dissolute youth who lived near him. For a long time he took no action in the hope that someone else would intervene, and finally people started to complain about the young man.

Malik then approached him and took him to task, asking him to reform. But the youth informed Malik that he was a favourite of the Sultan, and that nobody could stop him from doing whatever he liked.

Malik said that he would go to the Sultan; but the youth assured him that the ruler would never change his mind about him.

'In that case,' said Malik, 'I will report you to the Creator above.'

The young man said that God was far too forgiving to reproach him.

Malik was nonplussed, and he left the youth to himself; but presently his reputation became so bad that there was a public outcry against him. Malik set off to reprimand him again.

As he was walking to his house, however, he heard a voice from beyond call out:

'Do not touch my friend!'

Malik was astonished, and walked into the presence of the youth in a state of confusion.

As soon as he saw him, the profligate asked why he had come again.

Malik said, 'I cannot reproach you, but I must tell you what has happened.' And he reported the experience with the voice.

The evil-doer said, 'If he is my Friend, I will give all my

possessions to him.' Abandoning his wealth, he became a wanderer.

Malik Dinar met this man again one day in Mecca.

The youth said:

'I have come to see my Friend' — and he died.

Raised and Cast Down

A MAN on a camel passing the sage Zardalu shouted at the sight of such a humble one who was believed by his followers to be a great teacher:

'If the Teaching is designed to uplift man, why is it that so many men can be found who are cast down?'

Zardalu answered, without raising his head:

'If it were not for the Teaching, man would not, I agree, be cast down. He would be extinct.'

Perplexity

THERE was once a man who lived quietly in a certain place, not far from a mountain. He was well-behaved and refined, but the ordinary people did not see anything very remarkable about him. But he had an attractive manner and there was something about his kindness and understanding which made many people visit him and ask his advice.

Whenever anyone came to see him, he gave them advice. One, for instance, he told to open a shop, another to learn how to build rafts, a third he recommended to learn about the growing of plants and how gardens were maintained.

One day a number of people who had set out to try to find Truth paused in their journey and were talking to one another.

The first one said, 'I was able to bring the whole group safely across the treacherous torrent which we have just crossed because a certain man once recommended me to learn raft-building.'

The second man said, 'When, on this journey, we were all captured by brigands, I secured our release by showing the chief of the robbers how to cultivate his garden. I was able to do this because of the instructions given me by a certain man, who suggested to me that I learn about flowers and gardens.'

A third man said, 'We have escaped the terrors of wild animals during this journey because of the instructions given me by a certain man. He it was who, when I asked him what I should do in my life, said, "Learn how to overcome wild animals."'

And the same was true of all the other people in the caravan. When they compared notes, each discovered that he had been told one simple thing about how to progress in life, though few of them had realized how important to their survival it might become.

The guide who was with them on the journey said:

'Just remember that if you had not taken the advice of that man, none of you would be here; for there are many people who went to him for counsel, and who laughed at him or forgot his lessons, because they did not recognize that there could be any inner meaning in what he advised.'

When the travellers arrived at the end of their journey, they saw that their guide was the very same man who had lived at the bottom of the mountain, who had given them advice. They had hardly recovered from their amazement when he took them into the presence of Truth—and then they saw that Truth was nothing less than that very same man.

Then the travellers were perplexed, and their spokesman asked, 'Why, if you are the Truth, as we now all see, did you not tell us at the very beginning, so that we would have been spared this journey and all these discomforts?'

But, no sooner had these words been spoken, than they realized—because they had seen Truth—that they would never have been able to perceive Truth unless they had been through the three stages: the stage of advice and taking it, the stage of travel and applying their knowledge, and the stage of recognizing Truth itself.

They had been able to arrive at their destination only because something in their inner selves had been able to recognize, in the ordinary advice of the man at the foot of the mountain, some inner ringing of truth, some fragment of reality. In this way can man come to the recognition of the Absolute Truth.

Admonition to Disciples

Now that you have been enrolled in the ranks of the Seekers, it is more than ever likely that you will stumble: for, forgetting that self-esteem can manifest itself anywhere, you may think that you are immune from it.

Just as the gains of enlistment among the Friends are great, the requirements of the disciple are higher than is needed in ordinary affairs.

Hasan of Basra illustrated this with the following tale:*

'I saw a drunken man trying to walk through a marsh, and I said, "Take care that you do not sink, for that is a quagmire."

'The drunkard answered, "Hasan, if I am swallowed up, only I shall be the loser. Think of yourself instead: for if you sink, your followers will go with you." '

* Recorded in Tazkarat.

Hasan of Basra

HASAN of Basra relates:*

'I had convinced myself that I was a man of humility and less than humble in my thoughts and conduct to others.

'Then one day I was standing on the bank of a river when I saw a man sitting there. Beside him was a woman and before them was a wine-flask.

'I thought, "If only I could reform this man and make him like I am instead of the degenerate creature which he is!"

'At that moment I saw a boat in the river, beginning to sink. The other man at once threw himself into the water where seven people were struggling, and brought six of them safely to the bank.

'Then the man came up to me, and said:

' "Hasan, if you are a better man than me, in the Name of God save that other man, the last remaining one."

'I found that I could not even save one man, and he was drowned.

'Now this man said to me:

' "This woman here is my mother. This wine-flask has only water in it. This is how you judge, and this is what you are like."

'I threw myself at his feet and cried out:

' "As you have saved six out of these seven in peril, save me from drowning in pride disguised as merit!"

'The stranger said:

' "I pray that God may fulfil your aim." '

* Recorded in Tazkarat.

48

What to do

THE Sufi sage Abdulalim of Fez refused to teach, but from time to time would advise people about the way to proceed on the Path.

One day a disciple, who was both incapable of learning and regularly driven abnormal by attending 'mystical ceremonies', visited him. He asked:

'How can I best profit from the teachings of the sages?'

The Sufi said:

'I am happy to be able to tell you that I have an infallible method which corresponds to your capacity.'

'And what is that, if I am allowed to hear it?'

'Simply stop up your ears and think about radishes.'

'Before, during or after the lectures and exercises?'

'*Instead* of attending any of them.'

The Test

ABU NUJUM visited the monastery of a follower of Sufism, who was known as Pir-o-Murshid Partau-Gir Dalil.

Dalil said:

'See how in our Order we dwell upon the beauties of celestial love! See how we carry out great austerities and self-denial! See how we read the classics and repeat the sayings and emulate the doings of the Ancient Elect! See what repute we have attained, so that we are universally admired, held up as examples, are laying the foundation of a strong house indeed!'

Abu Nujum said nothing. He sent one of his disciples—Atiyya—to open a prayer-hall where continuous religious exercises were performed, in one quarter of Dalil's city. Many of Dalil's disciples, trained to devotions and craving yet more, deserted their master and streamed to this new saint. Then Abu Nujum commissioned an ignorant miscreant to start an etheric Tekkia, a special structure, among whose resplendent canopies were preached and recited intoxicatingly sublime words and poems of celestial love. Another section of Dalil's people flocked there, overcome by this wonder. Then Abu Nujum opened a school where rhythmic twirling was carried out, under the instruction of the blackest-hearted knave in Samarkand, and many of the disciples of Dalil, now converted to the new observances, professed themselves fulfilled by the wonderful experience of attendance there, some even believing that miracles were effected as a result. Not content with this, the relentless Abu Nujum instructed a narrow-minded cleric to recite, day and night, the sayings and doings of the ancient Masters, together with extensive recitations from the Sufi classics. Another portion of the unhappy Dalil's followers trooped to this holy man and drank in what he had to offer. The final experiment was the setting up of a House of Repetition, in which Abu Nujum offered harsh training in formidable austerities and insisted on great sacrifices from all comers. Within its walls jostled princes and peasants, rich and poor, merchants and officials, clamouring to be tested and made to suffer for a noble aim.

Out of many hundreds of Dalil's original disciples, three only now remained faithful to their teacher. Abu Nujum visited him in his monastery and said:

'I have done all I can to show yourself to you. Now it remains for you to test these three to see whether they are really followers of anything, or whether through habit and sentiment they remain with you, perhaps only in defiance of the general behaviour, as is to be expected from some under all circumstances.'

Dalil threw himself at the feet of the real Teacher and said:

'Now that I have learned that I am suffering from shallow vanity and that my disciples are deluded and desiring showmen, is there not just a particle of hope that I may follow you?'

Abu Nujum said:

'So long as you believe that you dislike vanity and obtain no pleasure from others relying upon you, you cannot. What we have to sell is entrusted to us by its owner. It is not fitting that we should sell it for such meagre coin as physical suffering, money which people want to give away to buy something, or sensual pleasure imagined to be service of God.'

Dalil said:

'But are we not told in our traditions that it is noble to sacrifice, for example?'

Abu Nujum said:

'Those remarks were originally addressed to people who had overcome vanity. If you have not done the first act, how can you hope to try to practise the second?'

It was this remarkable revelation which produced the real humility of Dalil, who afterwards became the true Guide of Turkestan.

The Hundred Books

ONE of the sheikhs of the Khwajagan (Masters) was told that he should appear within three months before the clerics and lawyers of Turkestan, in order to satisfy them that he was teaching in the realm of Shariat—the traditional law of Islam.

He offered to send his students to be examined as to whether they knew the holy books and the ceremonies, but the king answered that he was to be examined according to the regularity and propriety of his works, as all the men of thought are examined.

Now this sage had in fact written no books. Three hundred of his disciples were set to work to produce, within the time allowed, impeccable interpretation books of the law and customs.

When the confrontation came, the sage said to the assembled examiners:

'I have brought a hundred of the books which contain the teachings imparted to my followers. Should you wish to inspect the others, give us a little time, for the remainder of the thousand books into which our work is imprisoned exist only in the hearts of the disciples; but we can write them out for you here; and I have brought five hundred people to start the work immediately, should you so desire it.'

Vehicle

SOMEONE complained to a Sufi sage that the stories which he gave out were interpreted in one way by some people, and in other ways by others.

'That is precisely their value,' he said; 'surely you would not think much of even a cup out of which you could drink milk but not water, or a plate from which you could eat meat but not fruit? A cup and a plate are limited containers. How much more capable should language be to provide nutrition? The question is not "How many ways can I understand this, and why can I not see it in only one way?" The question is rather "Can this individual profit from what he is finding in the tales?" '

The Formula

A CERTAIN well-known teacher gave a disciple a formula and said:

'Repeat this on rising in the morning, at the middle of the day and in the evening. So long as you remain my faithful disciple, you may be sure that all your physical and worldly affairs will prosper.'

When he heard this, another follower of the same sage was anxious to be given the same treatment. The sage said to him:

'First of all, this is a selective prescription, and not everyone can benefit from it. Secondly, even if it were necessary to assess you, the manner in which you have approached me in this matter makes it impossible to give it to you.'

The disciple said:

'How would I have approached you, if I had been in the right state?'

The sage told him:

'Much more tentatively. I myself certainly care little about the manner of your asking. It is only a coincidence that the abruptness of your approach would have annoyed anyone with something to give of a more material sort.

'But you might be able to learn from your examination of your own manner—which should be neither abrupt nor fawning—that a mind such as yours is at the moment cannot receive and work with such an exercise.'

The Lives and Doings of the Masters

A DERVISH of the first rank was asked:

'Why is it that people spend so much time and effort studying the lives and doings of the Masters of the past, when their lives may have been misreported, and their doings may have been for effects to be seen at that time, and their words may be full of hidden meaning?'

He said:

'The purpose of such study is for the student to know what is said by and about the Masters. Some of this is useful on the ordinary level. Some will become plain as the disciple progresses. Some of it is cryptic, so that its understanding will come at the right moment, only when the Seeker is ready. Some is for the purpose of being interpreted by a teacher. Some of it is there to cause opposition from those who could not proceed along the Way, so that it will deter them from interfering with the People of the Path. Remember well that distaste for our work is usually a sign for us that such a person is shunning us because he is one whom we ourselves should shun.'

Change

PARTAU asked Rastgu:

'Why do the Sufi sheikhs work in so many different ways?'

Rastgu said:

'If a student thinks that it is possible to learn anything by merely memorizing, or simply making bodily movements, or only doing breathing exercises, or concentrating upon companionship with a sage—such a man is not a student at all. If a teacher thinks that he can convey the Teaching to anyone by making him confine himself to self-study, by insisting upon discipline or ceremonial only, it is as foolish as if the student refused to undergo any or all of these things.

'When studying the ways of the sages, a dervish must always remember that man learns in a host of ways to do ordinary things in the ordinary world. To expect to learn something higher with the few means which are used for teaching something lower is a mark of someone who has not become a student yet. In a guide, it is a mark of a repeater, not a teacher. It may be the mark of an imitation, but all will depend upon whether this man is a deputy of a sage or arrogant enough to imagine that imitation is teaching.'

Appetite

FIROZ was asked:

'The books and the very presence of a man of wisdom increase the appetite for learning in the public, and also in those who wish to understand the real meaning of man. Is it not harmful to excite the anticipation of those who may not be able to profit from the Teaching, and who are incapable of recognizing its beauty, meaning and significance?'

He said:

'Water will attract the greedy man, but that is no argument against water. There are greedy men who are excited at the sight of apricots. If they try to steal them, they may be punished. If their greed causes them to gobble them so that their stomachs cannot sustain the load, they become sick. The owner of the orchard does not become sick.'

The questioner continued:

'But in the interests of the thirsty man, could the water not be given to him in small amounts, so that he does himself no harm?'

Firoz said:

'Sometimes there is a kindly person present when he sees a crazed thirsty one, and he prevents him from killing himself through drinking too much. At other times, as you well know, the thirsty man comes across a well, and there is nobody there to prevent him destroying himself. Even if there were a well-meaning bystander, to say "Be careful!" the man crazed with thirst would thrust him aside and believe him to be his enemy.'

The questioner asked:

'Is there no way in which a person may be safeguarded against these perils?'

Firoz told him:

'If you can find anything in this life which is without any

danger of abuse and lacks risk for the stupid, tell me, and I shall myself spend all my time concentrating upon that thing. In the meantime learn, before it may be too late, that the guide exists because the path is rough. If you, so to speak, want to be able to breathe in without breathing out, or to waken up without facing the day—you are no Seeker, but a mere trumpery dilettante, and a hypocrite at that, for to call oneself something which one is not is contrary to the dignity of the people of dedication and straightforwardness.'

Oil, Water, Cotton

A CERTAIN man who was fond of studying all kinds of systems of thought wrote to a dervish Master* asking whether he could talk to him in order to make comparisons.

The dervish sent him a bottle with oil and water in it, and a piece of cotton wick. Enclosed in the package was this letter:

Dear friend, if you place the wick in the oil, you will get light when fire is applied to it. If you pour out the oil and put the wick in the water, you will get no light. If you shake up the oil and water and then place the wick in them, you will get a spluttering and a going out. There is no need to carry out this experiment through words and visits, when it can be done with such simple materials as these.

* Attributed to Abdul-Aziz of Mecca.

Sayed Sabir Ali-Shah

THE Sayed was asked, 'Why did Sheikh Attar write *Recapitulation of the Friends of God*?' He said, 'Because the Koran was no longer being experienced, but was being expounded.'

'And why did Maulana Rumi write the *Masnavi*?'

'Because the *Recapitulation* was not being read but was being memorized.'

'And who are the people who can interpret writings of the Sufis?'

'Those who do not need what they contain.'

'What are they called?'

'You could call them a very special sort of grocer. A grocer is a man who has more provisions than he needs for himself, so he sells them to others. We call them the *Pirs* (ancients) and *Murshids* (guides).'

In Mecca

JUNAID relates that he once saw a barber in Mecca shaving a rich man. A wandering dervish, he went up to the barber and asked him to shave him. The barber at once left his wealthy customer and shaved Junaid. Instead of asking for money, he gave him some.

Junaid resolved inwardly that whatever he might be given in charity that day he would take to the barber.

Not long afterwards, someone came up to the dervish and handed him a bag of gold. Junaid hurried to the barber's shop and offered it to the barber.

The barber said:

'Have you no shame in offering payment for something done for the sake of God?'

Halqavi

THEY asked Halqavi:

'What behaviour have you adopted during your life towards the people whom you have met, in order to determine their qualities?'

He said:

'I have generally acted in a submissive and humble manner. Those who became aggressive in response to my humility, I avoided as soon as I could. Those who respected me because of the humility of my appearance, I shunned as quickly.'

The Journeys of Kazwini

USEFUL men, carrying on useful work, do not become angry if they are called useless. But the useless who imagine that they are operating in a significant manner become greatly infuriated if this word is used about them.

'I visited', says Kazwini, 'one group of sincere-enough Sufis. They practised invocations and strummed music on strings.

'I listened to the discourses of eminent authorities, and attended the festivals of the Masters, living and dead.

'I donned the patched robe and begged from door to door, as recommended in the classics. I prayed, I fasted and I gave charity.

'I learned the intricate gyrations and litanies, and took part in the Stillness.

'I mastered the ability to contain the inner agitation.

'I learned how to erase my "I", and how to restore it, purged.

'Then I met the Proof himself. The Proof said to me:

' "What do you seek?"

'I said:

' "I seek the Master."

'The Proof said:

' "Had you asked for more action, I would have given it to you. But as you desire Truth, I shall conduct you to the Truth."

'He conveyed me to the Master. And the Master taught me what all the outwardness which I had studied really meant.

'When I returned to the world, none would listen, and the outwardness continues. As the Master predicted to me, it will continue until the end of time.'

Inconsistencies

A RARE writing by Rafik explains the purposeful reality behind outward inconsistency.

'Note well', he says, 'the people who express surprise at the inconsistencies which they find in dervish speech and action.

'Such people have not yet realized that the Path is followed by effective means, not by "sameness".

'If you find the externals and procedures of any Tekkia identical with any other, know that one of them at least is an imitation.

'The dervish who can only say the same thing to everyone at all times is not a teacher, Felicitous One!

'Children always like the things which are always the same.

'Those who prize and understand rarities seek uniqueness, do they not?—they do not seek sameness, but rather the reverse.

'Yet the shallow literalist acts and thinks like an undiscriminating infant. Except that he insists upon being treated not as an infant but as a connoisseur.'

A Report by Kirmani

THE Sufi monastery at Shishtout has a Tekkia hall with dazzlingly inlaid tiles of priceless worth.

For nearly three hundred years sheikhs, emirs, sultans and learned men flocked here to meditate and to sit with the Master of the Age.

But he had his own circle and carried out his own exercises in a rectangular room which looked like a kitchen.

That is why there is, in many a Tekkia, a spot known as the Hearth.

The Land of Truth

A CERTAIN man believed that the ordinary waking life, as people know it, could not possibly be complete.

He sought the real Teacher of the Age. He read many books and joined many circles, and he heard the words and witnessed the deeds of one master after another. He carried out the commands and spiritual exercises which seemed to him to be most attractive.

He became elated with some of his experiences. At other times he was confused; and he had no idea at all of what his stage was, or where and when his search might end.

This man was reviewing his behaviour one day when he suddenly found himself near the house of a certain sage of high repute. In the garden of that house he encountered Khidr, the secret guide who shows the way to Truth.

Khidr took him to a place where he saw people in great distress and woe, and he asked who they were. 'We are those who did not follow real teachings, who were not true to our undertakings, who revered self-appointed teachers,' they said.

Then the man was taken by Khidr to a place where everyone was attractive and full of joy. He asked who they were. 'We are those who did not follow the real Signs of the Way,' they said.

'But if you have ignored the Signs, how can you be happy?' asked the traveller.

'Because we chose happiness instead of Truth,' said the people, 'just as those who chose the self-appointed chose also misery.'

'But is happiness not the ideal of man?' asked the man.

'The goal of man is Truth. Truth is more than happiness. The man who has Truth can have whatever mood he wishes, or none,' they told him. 'We have pretended that Truth is happiness, and happiness Truth, and people have believed us, therefore you, too, have until now imagined that happiness must be the same as Truth. But happiness makes you its prisoner, as does woe.'

Then the man found himself back in the garden, with Khidr beside him.

'I will grant you one desire,' said Khidr.

'I wish to know why I have failed in my search and how I can succeed in it,' said the man.

'You have all but wasted your life,' said Khidr, 'because you have been a liar. Your lie has been in seeking personal gratification when you could have been seeking Truth.'

'And yet I came to the point where I found you,' said the man, 'and that is something which happens to hardly anyone at all.'

'And you met me,' said Khidr, 'because you had sufficient sincerity to desire Truth for its own sake, just for an instant. It was that sincerity, in that single instant, which made me answer your call.'

Now the man felt an overwhelming desire to find Truth, even if he lost himself.

Khidr, however, was starting to walk away, and the man began to run after him.

'You may not follow me,' said Khidr, 'because I am returning to the ordinary world, the world of lies, for that is where I have to be, if I am to do my work.'

And when the man looked around him again, he realized that he was no longer in the garden of the sage, but standing in the Land of Truth,

Language

RIFAI was asked:

'Why do you have to use so many analogies when you are talking of higher understanding. Can we not speak in plain language of such things?'

He said:

'This is an example of "sublime ignorance producing co rect information". If there were no people who did not know things, we would not be able to discern as to who is wise. Know, therefore, that language is itself an analogy. Every word and phrase, every letter, is an analogy.

'In words we cannot speak of higher things directly, since no language encompasses higher things and not lower things as well.'

Almost an Apple

NAJRANI said:

'If you say that you can "nearly understand", you are talking nonsense.'

A theologian who liked this phrase asked:

'Can you give us an equivalent of this in ordinary life?'

'Certainly,' said Najrani; 'it is equivalent to saying that something is "almost an apple".'

Etiquette

AN inquirer asked Sayed Khidr Rumi:

'Is there anything which can be called the best and also the worst of human institutions?'

He said:

'Yes, indeed. There is such a thing, and its name is "etiquette".

'The advantage of etiquette and conduct is that it enables the Wise to approach the student without being jeered at, and it makes possible the search by the student without people thinking him ridiculous.

'The disadvantage of etiquette which makes it the worst of human institutions is that it enables the ignorant to erect their own rules of what is permissible in thought and conduct and what is not. If such people decide that there are certain things which should never be thought or done, then they can effectively prevent the transmission of knowledge.'

The inquirer asked:

'May I have an instance of how this happens in our Teaching?'

Sayed Khidr Rumi said:

'It has become customary for people, when they read prescribed books and accounts of the doings of the Masters, to say, "This is an analogy which does not apply to me." It also enables them to say, "This is an encounter with a stupid man. *I* could never think like the man in the tale; therefore the Teacher is in this instance dealing with a completely different type of person." The reality is that such a person is always the one most in need of teaching, while he is unaware of it.

'There is the story of the dog who was distressed when a man shouted at him, saying, "Look at that mangy creature!" The dog, instead of looking for a sage who would cure his mange, jumped into a pool of water and came out dripping wet. He ran up to the man, wagging his tail, as if to say, "Look, my coat is changed, it is all dampness where before it was a dusty mat!" The man started to curse him even more strongly, because he did not want the dog to shake the water off all over him.

'The dog became convinced that the man was irrational, while it was simply a matter that the one did not understand the other. In the instance of the acts related of the Wise, the doggishness in the student must realize that the sage is talking about a real, not an illusory, improvement in his state.'

Reactions

A CERTAIN philosopher said to a Sufi sage:

'You must always deal with a farmer, say, or a soldier, or a merchant, differently.'

The Sufi disagreed, saying, 'People behave in the same way if you approach them in the same way.'

The Sufi sent the rich man to live in a hovel, and a farmer to visit a friend of his who lived in a palace, and a soldier to associate with the friends of a rich merchant.

They all became depressed in their new surroundings, and all sent him messages, saying, 'We wanted to study under you, and we find ourselves depressed and making no progress in our studies.'

Now the Sufi showed the philosopher these letters, and remarked, 'I can find no difference in the behaviour of these three men, all different and all in different surroundings.'

He sent a message to the three, in which he said, 'I wanted to test your resolution, whether you would flourish if you were placed somewhere which you did not expect.'

All three of them met later at the home of the Sufi, and agreed among themselves that the Sufi, having failed to influence them in some manner, was now trying to explain his conduct in a manner which would impress them.

The philosopher, invited to see the Sufi, after examining the three men, said, 'I admit that they have all shown the same kind of behaviour. But in presenting this demonstration to me, you have violated your own principles of teaching: for you have preferred victory in debate to what you people call real teaching. You have caused these three men to distrust all Sufis, and hence placed them outside the realm of your teaching.'

The Sufi said, 'On the contrary, it is you who have failed to observe that I chose, in the first place, candidates who would not in any case have been accessible to higher understanding. There cannot therefore have been any waste of potentiality.'

The philosopher, however, persisted. 'If you have been working with people who have no prospects, you have undoubtedly violated another principle of the people of your school. This, I must remind you, is your contention that "Everything that a Sufi does is significantly connected with the higher aim." '

The Sufi said, 'You are again wrong, because you choose your own interpretations, preferring to ignore the operation of the Teaching. I shall have to explain. The demonstration, providing that its lessons are learnt, will enable others to learn and to avoid similar mistakes. This is an essential part of the higher aim. Words are useless by themselves; what the words can do is the very reverse of useless.'

Motivation

A WOMAN was sitting by the roadside, weeping most bitterly at the grave of her daughter. She was the object of sympathy and concern to everyone who saw her. Yet Sheikh Attar observes that those who sympathized with her were themselves in a worse case.

The woman, as a wayfarer points out, unlike a thousand other people around, at least knew the cause of her grief and the object from which she had been separated.

Man is in a similar condition of estrangement—as it were from his family—but does not know it. All he knows is that he is unhappy, and he has to invent reasons to which he then attributes his misery.

Three Interpretations

THREE dervishes who had resolved to find Truth arrived at the home of one of the great teachers.*

They asked him to help them; and for answer he took them into his garden. Picking up a stick of dead wood, he walked from one bed of flowers to another. striking off the blooms of the tallest of the plants.

When they returned to the house, the sage seated himself among his students and asked, 'What was the meaning of my actions? Whichever of you can interpret them aright will be accepted for the Teaching.'

The first dervish said, 'My interpretation of the lesson is "people who imagine that they know more than others may have to suffer a levelling in the Teaching."'

The second dervish said, 'My understanding of the actions is "things which are beautiful in appearance may be unimportant in the totality."'

The third dervish said, 'I would describe what you did as indicating "a dead thing, even a stick of repetitious knowledge, can still harm what is alive."'

The Master said, 'You are all enrolled, for between you meanings are shared. Not one of you knows all; what all of you have is not complete; but what each of you says is correct.'

* Reputedly Mir Alisher Nawai.

Farmyard

A CERTAIN teacher of the highest rank was also a farmer. He had written many books and lectures. One day a man who had read them all, and imagined himself to be a Seeker, called to discuss higher matters with him.

'I have read all your books,' said the visitor, 'and I agree with some and not with others. In some, again, I agree with some parts and do not understand other parts. Some books I like better than others.'

The farmer-sage took his guest into the farmyard, where the animals and fodder were abundant. Then he said, 'I am a farmer, a producer of food. Do you see those carrots and those apples? Some people like the one, others, the other. Do you see the animals? Some people have seen them all, but have their preferences— for riding, for breeding and for food. Some like hens, others like goats.

'The common denominator is not liking or disliking. The common factor is nutrition. It is all *food*.'

Streaky Sand

THERE was once a woman who abandoned the religion in which she had been brought up. She left the ranks of the atheists, too, and joined another faith. Then she became convinced of the truth of yet another.

Each time she changed her beliefs, she imagined that she had gained something, but not quite enough. Each time she entered a new fold, she was welcomed, and her recruitment was regarded as a good thing and a sign of her sanity and enlightenment.

Her inward state, however, was one of confusion. At length she heard of a certain celebrated teacher,* and she went to see him. After he had listened to her protestations and ideas, he said, 'Return to your home. I shall send you my decision in a message.'

Soon afterwards the woman found a disciple of the sheikh at the door. In his hand was a packet from his Master. She opened it, and saw that it contained a glass bottle, half-full with three layers of packed sand—black, red and white—held down by a wad of cotton. On the outside was written: 'Remove the cotton and shake the bottle to see what you are like.'

She took the wadding out, and shook the sand in the bottle. The different coloured grains of sand mixed together, and all that she was left with was—a mass of greyish sand.

* Traditionally Imam Jafar Sadik.

To Seek to Learn to Seek

RAIS EL-SULUK taught his disciples:

'I have only one lesson. When you have learned this, you will be able to learn another.

'I searched everywhere for spirituality until I understood that it was not to be found in any of the places where the unworthy seek it.

'My Master, Hakim Anis, taught me that I must learn how to be worthy to seek.

'Seeking without worthiness is arrogance concealed.

'I asked the Hakim where I should go to find knowledge and not opinion.

'Then he taught me what I did not want to learn, in a way I did not want. He taught me how to seek knowledge.'

The Necessity for the Teaching

MARUF, son of Zayd, was asked:

'Why is the Teaching not offered to the people of so many countries where, through their material advancement, the people could help the progress of the Work?'

He said:

'Where a people have no capacity, and where the activity has no teachers, there is no advantage in material or other advancement. You can make no swords where there is no iron.

'One day, you will recall from the *Munaqib*, Muinudin requested Maulana Rumi to give his son "special mystical training by projection". Rumi answered, "The load which forty men pull—cannot be sustained by one."

'The mystical force can be perceived by men, and not by a man alone. Where there is no quantity, there can be no sharing.

'If you had a camel-load of halwa, you would need the exact number of boxes to put it in before you discharged your load.'

The questioner was not pleased with this answer, and he said:

'The sage has failed to note that we are not merchants of halwa!'

The sage, however, said, gently, 'If you were, you would understand what I mean.'

Observing One's Own Opinions

'FOR months', recalls the sage Hakim Masum, 'I was made by my Master, Khwaja Alam Shah, to write letters to his dictation and to keep notes of what he said and thought.

'When I saw him writing, I could see that he wrote faster and much more beautifully than I. Many of the things which I wrote were so badly done that there was difficulty in reading them.

'One day he said:

' "I have been trying to give you the exercise you needed. If you improve your speed and calligraphy, so much the better. If you think I am too illiterate or lazy to do my own work, you have a chance immediately afterwards of observing your own opinions, and seeing that they are opinions. And seeing that opinions, if they are just the ones that suit you, distort your senses." '

Great Worth

A MAN came to Bahaudin Shah and said:

'First I followed this teacher, and then that one. Next I studied these books, and then those. I feel that although I know nothing of you and your teachings, this experience has been slowly preparing me to learn from you.'

The Shah answered:

'Nothing you have learned in the past will help you here. If you are to stay with us, you will have to abandon all pride in the past. That is a form of self-congratulation.'

The man exclaimed:

'This is, to me, the proof that you are the great, the real and the true Teacher! For none whom I have met in the past has dared to deny the value of what I had studied before!'

Bahaudin said:

'This feeling is in itself unworthy. In accepting me so enthusiastically, and without understanding, you are flattering yourself that you have perceptions which are in fact lacking in you.

'You are still, in effect, saying, "I am of some worth, because I have recognized Bahaudin as a great man."'

Analogy

A CERTAIN important man of learning said to a Sufi:

'Why do you Sufis always use analogies? Such forms are good enough for the ignorant, but you can speak clearly to people of sense.'

The Sufi said:

'Experience shows, alas, that it is not a matter of the ignorant and the wise. It is a matter that those who are most in need of a certain understanding, or even a certain part of understanding, are always the least able to accept it without an analogy. Tell them directly and they will prevent themselves perceiving its truth.'

Lucky People

ISHAN TURKI sent a disciple on a long journey, quite alone. His instructions were to seek out people who regarded themselves as lucky, and only to spend time with them, to stay with them, to eat with them, to support himself by working for them.

When he was asked why he did this, the Master said:

'All people who regard themselves as lucky have the kind of calmness that I wished to expose my disciple to. The best way to enable him to find the kind of people was to describe the main characteristic which such a person would have.

'If I had asked him to find people with calm, he would not have known how to do it.'

A questioner asked:

'But what if he had met a genuinely "lucky" man, who *knew* he was lucky, and not one who just imagined it because he was calm and optimistic?'

The Ishan said:

'Such a man would have been a teacher and a sage. He would have known how to deal with my disciple, to further his progress, and thus he would have worked to the advantage of all of us.'

Value for Money

AWAD AFIFI had a book in which he had written the accounts of conversations with sages and philosophers during twenty years of travels and studies.

One day a scholar called to see him and asked if he could make a copy of the book.

'Yes,' said Awad, 'you may certainly do so. I will charge you, however, a thousand gold pieces for the service.'

'That is a tremendous sum to pay for something that you have here, which I am not even going to deplete by copying,' said the scholar, 'and, besides, it is unworthy to charge for knowledge.'

'I make no charge for knowledge itself,' said Awad, 'for knowledge is not in books, only some of the ways to gain it. As for the thousand gold pieces: I intend to spend them on the travel expenses of pupils who cannot afford to travel. And as for the greatness of the sum: I have spent fifty thousand on my travels, plus twenty years of my life. Perhaps you might care to let me know what that amounts to?'

The Man Who Gave More —
and Less

INQILABI said:

'I went to many a respected Master, each strongly revered by his following, each revered by me.

'Then I found a different one. He told me so many things I never imagined that I saw him as generous beyond all others.

'But when, through his aid, I arrived at full knowledge of the Secret I realized that it was all the others who had been much more generous. They had told me all they knew, but it had been useful in appearance and not in reality.

'Generosity without substance is nobility, not sustenance.

'Why did he not give me yet more of what he had?

'I would have charged him with this parsimony; but yet I could not have, for it was only at the end that I realized that—as with a child—though instructing me little compared to what there was, he had guided me aright. He had given me what was needful, not what was remarkable.'

When Even Kings are Weak . . .

SHAH FIROZ, who is remembered as the teacher of many very distinguished Sufis, was often asked during his lifetime why he did not teach them faster.

He said, 'Because even the most dedicated will, until a certain point of understanding, not be teachable at all. He is here in the flesh, but absent in every other way.'

He also recited this tale.

There was once a king who wanted to become a Sufi. The Sufi whom he approached about the matter said, 'Majesty, you cannot study with the Elect until you can overcome heedlessness.'

'Heedlessness!' said the king. 'Am I not heedful of my religious obligations? Do I not look after the people? Whom can you find in all my realm who has a complaint against me on the grounds of heedlessness?'

'That is precisely the difficulty,' said the Sufi, 'because heedfulness is so marked in some things, people imagine that it must be a part of their texture.'

'I cannot understand that sort of remark,' said the king, 'and perhaps you will regard me as unsuitable because I cannot fathom your riddles.'

'Not at all,' said the Sufi; 'but a would-be disciple cannot really have a debate with his prospective teacher. Sufis deal in knowledge, not argument. But I will give you a demonstration of your heedlessness, if you will carry out a test and do what I ask in respect to it.'

The king agreed to take the test, and the Sufi told him to say 'I believe you' to everything which should be said to him in the ensuing few minutes.

'If that is a test, it is easy enough to start becoming a Sufi,' said the king.

Now the Sufi started the test. He said:

'I am a man from beyond the skies.'

'I believe you,' said the king.

The Sufi continued:

'Ordinary people try to gain knowledge, Sufis have so much that they try not to use it.'

'I believe you,' said the king.

Then the Sufi said:

'I am a liar.'

'I believe you,' said the king.

The Sufi went on:

'I was present when you were born.'

'I believe you,' said the king.

'And your father was a peasant,' said the Sufi.

'That is a lie!' shouted the king.

The Sufi looked at him sorrowfully and said:

'Since you are so heedless that you cannot for one minute remember to say "I believe you" without some prejudice coming into play, no Sufi would be able to teach you anything.'

Conversion

KHWAJA AHRAR'S reputation had grown so great that many people flocked to enrol themselves as his supporters, whether he wanted them or not.

One day he heard that four particularly obnoxious individuals were on their way to see him, determined to be able to say that they had become followers of the Lord of the Free.

He immediately made inquiries about these people's likes and dislikes. When they arrived, they found that he was wearing a red cap, talking immoderately, eating sweetmeats and claiming that he was unable to resist opium.

They spent less than half an hour in his presence, and never spoke about him again.

Astrology

A CERTAIN respected thinker and teacher had written a book on astrology. Some people said that he must be a magician or insane; others believed that this action had shown that there was truth in astrology.

Ultimately a dervish who had travelled many miles to see the sage asked him about the problem, saying, 'Surely astrological work is inconsistent with the Path of the Wise, and the Work of the Elect?'

The sage answered:

'I make absolutely sure that all my pupils study my book on astrology. In this way they are able to understand that astrology does not work. When they are completely skilled in the art, I make them interpret horoscopes. These we compare, and we always find such discrepancies in interpretation, when properly tested, that it becomes self-evident that the system is useful only for imaginings.'

The visitor said:

'Could you not simply tell them that astrology is not a true science, as others do?'

'Firstly,' said the sage, 'if the telling had been effective when done by others, who would still believe in astrology? When did telling equal understanding? Secondly, when you have thoroughly investigated one superstition, you are unlikely to be able to sustain, or adopt, another.'

'So it is not astrology in particular which you seek to dispose of?'

'No. Astrology is one of the easiest absurdities to study, because its practitioners have allowed themselves to be pinned down to rules.'

I'll Make You Remember

ONE day Latif the Thief ambushed the commander of the Royal Guard, captured him and took him to a cave.

'I am going to say something that, no matter how much you try, you will be unable to forget,' he told the infuriated officer.

Latif made his prisoner take off all his clothes. Then he tied him, facing backwards, on a donkey.

'You may be able to make a fool of me,' screamed the soldier, 'but you'll never make me think of something if I want to keep it out of my mind.'

'You have not yet heard the phrase which I want you to remember,' said Latif. 'I am turning you loose now, for the donkey to take back to town. And the phrase is:

' "I'll catch and kill Latif the Thief, if it takes me the rest of my life!" '

The Next Generation

THERE was once a philosopher who insisted on his rights when ownership of a certain well was disputed. He was adamant about his proprietorship, too, of a clump of palm trees. In a third case he became notorious for insisting that he was the sole owner of a certain rectangular house.

He won all these cases, but people said to him, 'How could a man of detachment place such value upon transitory objects such as these?'

He said:

'The question asked from suspicion and hostility has driven its answer into the next generation.'

Nobody could understand this, and they therefore imagined that he was deliberately trying to confuse.

In the next generation, however, deceitful advisers trying to usurp the property of a devout minor said to him:

'Yield your property to us, for you are a pious man—things of this world are of no account.'

'What is my property?' he asked them.

'A long house, some palm trees and a well,' they said.

'Then I will abide by the precedent of the Wise. Look up the writings and doings of such-and-such an acknowledged sage,' he said—and gave the name and quoted the collection where were recorded the actions of the philosopher.

If He Looks Good, He is Good

A MAN went to Imam Zainulabidin and said:

'I recognize you as my leader and teacher, and I beg to be allowed to learn from you.'

The Imam asked:

'Why do you believe that I am a leader and a teacher?'

The newcomer answered:

'I have searched all my life, and I have never found anyone with such a reputation for kindness and warmth and goodly appearance.'

The Imam wept and said:

'Dear friend, how frail a thing is man, and in what danger! The very reputation and actions you attribute to me are shared with some of the worst people in the world. If all men judge only on appearances, every devil will be thought a saint, and every superior man could be made out to be an enemy of humanity.'

Ruling and Ruled

A DERVISH was asked:

'Which is better, to be a ruler or to be ruled?'

He said:

'To be ruled. The person being ruled is constantly informed by the ruler that he is wrong, whether he is or not. This gives him a chance to improve by studying himself—for sometimes he is indeed wrong.

'The administrator, however, almost always imagines that he himself or his regulations are right; so he has little opportunity to examine his behaviour.

'That is why the ruled eventually become rulers, and rulers fall to the status of the ruled.'

He was asked:

'Then what is the purpose of the promotion of the ruled and the downfall of the ruler, just repeated again and again?'

He said:

'So that rulers may learn what ruling really entails, and the ruled may learn how good, as well as how bad, they really are.'

'But,' said the questioner, 'how can a man have a chance to benefit from this if it takes generations for the ruler to become the ruled and the ruled the ruler?'

'It does not take generations. It happens many times in every man and woman's life. The development which you see throughout the generations is simply an illustration of this.'

Hariri the Good Man

HARIRI always tried to behave in as exemplary a manner as possible. He acquired such a reputation for correct conduct that a certain merchant who had to go on a journey chose him as the obvious person with whom to entrust the welfare of his beautiful slave-girl.

But Hariri developed a passion for the girl. He went to Haddad, his Sufi preceptor, and asked for his advice. Haddad said:

'Go to Yusuf, son of Hussain.'

When Hariri approached the place where Yusuf was to be found, people said:

'Do not go near the Son of Hussain, pious man, for he has a bad reputation, is a heretic and a wine-drinker.'

Not believing this, Hariri arrived at Yusuf's door, where he saw, sure enough, Yusuf was sitting with a young boy and a flask of wine.

Hariri at once said to Yusuf:

'What is the meaning of this behaviour?'

Yusuf said, reading his thoughts:

'I behave like this in appearance, because it prevents people entrusting their beautiful slaves to my keeping.'

Camlet

A VERY forthright and extremely intelligent man, using the dervish name of Fakir Khamlet, arrived in Samarkand. Khamlet means, in English, the type of woollen cloth formerly known as camlet.

As was the custom, he addressed the public in the Friday Market on all manner of subjects. He rapidly acquired a reputation as a learned man, and several of the long-established scholars of the city went to visit him in the humble caravanserai where he lived.

One said: 'We would like to know the school of thought to which you belong, and the name of your teacher.'

He said: 'I belong to the Asmania School, and my teacher is none other than Faqih Kawkab, son of el-Utarid, of the Falak, the Elevated Noble.'

The scholars had never heard of this celebrated man, but could discern from his name that he was a lawyer, probably a juristconsult, and had certainly been ennobled.

They said:

'Though the reputation of the Lawyer Kawkab is not entirely unknown in this remote place, yet his books and disciples have not yet reached us in great numbers. So we applaud your devotion to his name, and your modesty in acknowledging your teacher, not coming here pretending that you alone are master of your thoughts.'

So Fakir Khamlet was accepted on this intellectual pedigree.

Some years afterwards, however, a traveller arrived in Samarkand from Yemen, saying:

'I seek Faqih Kawkab, son of el-Utarid of the Falak. Has anyone seen him in Samarkand? He is the greatest of our teachers, and sometimes calls himself Khamlet, and comes from a place called Asman.'

Respect

EL-AMUDI allowed the kitchen-boy to receive his guests. The water-pots in the guest-house were often empty. When distinguished visitors came to the house, the sage seldom talked to them on any serious subject at first. Once he had all the robes worn by a group of prominent clerics sprayed with muddy water.

Some showed a taste for this conduct, and El-Amudi used to send such people away as soon as possible.

Others often said:

'We have never been treated with such disrespect!'

El-Amudi used to say to such people:

'You failed to inform me that you came for respect. I have never offered it, since I have been too deeply occupied in offering knowledge. Respect, you will have to learn, is available from every shopkeeper and everyone who has expectations from you.'

The Legend of the Three Men

ONCE upon a time there were three men, who went on a journey together.

They came upon a small coin by the roadside. As they had no other money, each started to argue with the others as to what they should buy with it.

The first man said, 'I want something sweet to eat!'

'No,' said the second, 'I want several sweet things to eat.'

'No!' said the third. 'I want something to quench my thirst.'

A wise man passing by stopped and they asked him to adjudicate between them.

'Choose,' they said, 'which of us should have his desire.'

'I will do better than that,' said the sage, 'for I can undertake to satisfy you all.'

He went to a near-by shop and with the money bought a bunch of grapes, which he divided between them.

'But this is something sweet to eat,' said the first.

'But this is several sweet things to eat,' said the second man.

'But this is something with which to quench my thirst,' said the third man.

Mystery

TALIB said:

'People who know nothing, or know very little and should be studying instead of teaching, are fond of creating an air of mystery. They may foster rumours about themselves and pretend that they do things for some secret reason. They always strive to increase the sense of mystery.

'But this is mystery for itself, not as the outer manifestation of inner knowledge.

'The people who really know the inner secrets generally look and behave like ordinary people.

'So the ones who increase the air of mystery may be like the spider's web, they only catch flies. Are you, like the fly, a spider's dinner?'

Merchant of Secrets

A MYSTICAL Master, as soon as he attained the secret knowledge of the Inner Truth which few people find, settled in Basra.

There he started a business and over the years his affairs prospered.

A dervish who had known him in former years and yet was himself still on the road of the Seekers called upon him one day.

'How sad to see that you have abandoned the Search and the Mystic Way,' said the dervish. The merchant-sage smiled, but said nothing on this subject.

The dervish passed on his way, and often afterwards spoke in his lectures of the one-time Sufi who had settled for the lower aim of commerce, being, it seemed, lacking in the necessary resolution to complete the journey.

But this wanderer at length fell in with Khidr, the secret Guide, and begged him to direct him to the Sage of the Epoch from whom he could obtain enlightenment.

Khidr said:

'Go and sit at the feet of such-and-such a merchant, performing whatever menial task he needs done.'

The dervish was amazed. 'But how can he be one of the Elect, let alone the Great Teacher of the Age?' he stammered.

'Because,' said Khidr, 'when he gained illumination he also achieved objective knowledge of the world. He saw clearly for the first time that saintly behaviour attracts the greedy posing as the spiritual, and repels the sincere who have no taste for outwardness. I showed him how religious teachers may be drowned by their followers. So he teaches in secret, and looks, to the superficial, like a mere merchant.'

Distant Projection

I T is related that a merchant once made a journey of six months' duration from Africa to study with Jalaludin Rumi.

He took a room at the Serai in Konia, sent his servant to announce his arrival, and waited for the summons of the Maulana.

Before the servant had arrived at Rumi's house, however, a dervish who was serving in the Serai's kitchen said to the merchant:

'Why are you here?'

'I am here', said the merchant, 'to glimpse the blessed countenance of our Master, Jalaludin of Balkh.'

'And how much has it cost you to come this long distance, friend?'

'Over a thousand gold pieces.'

'How remarkable,' said the dervish, 'for yesterday night at the Maulana's meeting I heard him say something which could apply to you.'

The merchant was excited and asked:

'Please tell me at once, omitting no detail.'

'What he said,' the dervish told him, 'was this: "If I only had a thousand gold pieces such as some people throw away for the vanity of a journey to give to the deserving, I would be able to spare the effort to send mystical projection to a certain merchant of Africa, who needs it. But I am wholly occupied in the affairs of the welfare of the needy. Even if that merchant were to come here, he would be unable to receive the *Baraka* (sanctity). But if he did, he would no doubt be satisfied with the self-esteem, the pride at the journey and the sacrifices, and he would think that that was spiritual progress." '

Imam Baqir

IMAM MUHAMMED BAQIR is said to have related this illustrative fable:

'Finding I could speak the language of ants, I approached one and inquired, "What is God like? Does he resemble the ant?"'

'He answered, "God! No, indeed—we have only a single sting but God, He has *two*!"'

Ajnabi

ioioioioioioioioioioioioioioioioioioioioioioioioioioioioi

THE Sufi Master Ajnabi said:

'Write to Mulla Firoz and tell him that I have no time to engage him in correspondence, and therefore have nothing to say to his letter.'

The disciple Amini said:

'Is it your intention to annoy him with this letter?'

Ajnabi said:

'He has been annoyed by some of my writings. This annoyance has caused him to write to me. My purpose in writing the passage which angers him was to anger such as he.'

Amini said:

'And this letter will anger him further?'

Ajnabi said:

'Yes. When he was enraged at what I wrote, he did not observe his own anger, which was my intention. He thought that he was observing me, whereas he was only feeling angry. Now I write again, to arouse anger, so that he will see that he is angry. The objective is for the man to realize that my work is a mirror in which he sees himself.'

Amini said:

'The people of the ordinary world always regard those who cause anger as ill-intentioned.'

Ajnabi said:

'The child may regard the adult who tries to remove a thorn from his hand as ill-intentioned. Is that a justification for trying to prevent the child from growing up?'

Amini said:

'And if the child harbours a grudge against the adult who removes the thorn?'

Ajnabi said:

'The child does not really harbour that grudge, because something in him knows the truth.'

Amini asked him:

'But what happens if he never gets to know himself, and yet continues to imagine that others are motivated by personal feelings?'

Ajnabi said:

'If he never gets to know himself, it makes no difference as to what he thinks of other people, because he can never have any appreciation of what other people are really like.'

Amini asked:

'Is it not possible instead of arousing anger a second time to explain that the original writing was composed for this purpose, and to invite the Mulla to review his previous feelings?'

Ajnabi said:

'It is possible to do this, but it will have no effect. Rather it will have an adverse effect. If you tell the man your reason he will imagine that you are excusing yourself, and this will arouse in him sentiments which are harmful only to him. Thus, by explaining you are actually acting to his detriment.'

Amini said:

'Are there no exceptions to this rule, that man must learn through realizing his own state, and that his state cannot be explained to him?'

Ajnabi said:

'There are exceptions. But if there were enough exceptions to make any difference to the world, we would not by now have any Mulla Firozes left.'

Rahimi

In a private debate the scholar Salih Awami said to Sufi Rahimi:

'What you have just said lacks references and proofs through quotations from ancient authority.'

'Not at all,' said Rahimi, 'for I have them all here, chapter and verse.'

The scholar went away, saying, 'That was what I wanted to know.'

The next day he made his famous speech on Rahimi which began:

'The lecture which you are about to hear from Sheikh Rahimi lacks conviction. Why, he is so unsure of himself that he has actually adduced written proofs and authorities to what he says.'

Reading

NAWAB Jan Fishan Khan was asked:

'Why did his teacher not allow Rumi to study his father's own works? Surely nothing but good can come of the study of something good?'

Jan Fishan said:

'There were two reasons. First, that for every person there is an interpretation. If he is likely to make his own interpretation, he may follow the wrong track. As an example, if you have a child read a law-book, he will misinterpret the parts of the law which deal with matters which he has not yet reached in his experience.

'Secondly, books of higher learning are written in order to correspond with the needs of the time, place and people by whom they have to be read. If, for instance, you read Chinese books on dyeing, you may become a Chinese dyer—though there may be no demand for the style of dyeing done in China. Similarly, if the people of a certain place have reached a stage beyond that which is, in part, represented by earlier books, to make them concentrate upon these parts will hold them back.

'You should be thoroughly familiar with the recommended works. The meaning of them, however, requires a guide.'

Haji Bektash Wali

ASKED the question, 'Why do all the Paths differ?' Bektash said:

'Shoot an arrow at a target. To do this you must have an arrow and a target and a man to shoot. These are the elements which make up the action. They are called a school.

'But if the aim is to strike one object with another, there are a thousand ways of doing it. Only the shallow will think that arrow-shooting is the only way of hitting one thing with another. This is the Inner Way.'

He continued, 'All you have to do is to realize this.'

'But,' his inquirer persisted, 'how are we to know what is the way for us?'

'The people who pretend that you will know the most suitable method for yourself are the ones who pretend that what you like is what you need. Man probably does not know the way for himself. He needs someone to arrange the circumstances—such as finding two surfaces and aligning them so that they "collide", in the analogy of the arrow and the target.'

The Book of Nonsense

SHEIKH ABU-ALI of Yemen spoke one day of nonsensical books being attractive because they were nonsense. 'There are many such books,' he said.

A student wondered whether it were possible to have a demonstration of such an effect. Reading his thoughts although not a word had been spoken, the Sheikh wrote a 'mysterious book of symbols' which he showed to this youth, and then sent to China.

Three years later, Indians began to appear with the 'Ancient Chinese Book of Truth', claiming that it had worked miracles and would answer their questions. Abu-Ali would never discuss this marvellous book with them.

One day one of his disciples wondered what the effect of the book would be, other than as a demonstration for Abu-Ali's immediate circle.

Again, the Sheikh answered the unuttered thought.

'The "Ancient Chinese Book of Truth"', he said, 'in reality gives all who are confronted with it a chance to exercise an inner discrimination. They are given an opportunity, through confrontation, to assess inwardly whether or not this thing is a toy.

'Its great value for real Seekers is that they can see that the people who are interested in this book are people whom we can avoid, for they would waste our time and misinterpret our work.'

Shakir Amali

PEOPLE seek teachers and teaching in order to find something that they do not know already. In reality, however, teachers and teachings exist to help people to apply and practise, not to amuse or give experience that must be new.

Since men in general do not know this, it is not surprising that they do not know what they have found, and try to find what is of no use to them.

It is also possible that things which seem 'new' to people are the last things that they need for the purpose of improving them.

You will know the seeker of sensations because he is attracted by the new or mysterious. You will know the real student because he seeks whatever there is to be found.

How and What to Understand

THIS interchange between the Sufi mystic Simab and a noble-
man named Mulakab is preserved in oral transmission as a
dialogue often staged by wandering dervishes:

Mulakab: 'Tell me something of your philosophy, so that I
may understand.'

Simab: 'You cannot understand unless you have experienced.'

Mulakab: 'I do not have to understand a cake, to know
whether it is bad.'

Simab: 'If you are looking at a good fish and you think that
it is a bad cake, you need to understand less, and to understand
it better, more than you need anything else.'

Mulakab: 'Then why do you not abandon books and lectures, if experience is the necessity?'

Simab: 'Because "the outward is the conductor to the inward". Books will teach you something of the outward aspects
of the inward, and so will lectures. Without them, you would
make no progress.'

Mulakab: 'But why should we not be able to do without
books?'

Simab: 'For the same reason that you cannot think without
words. You have been reared on books, your mind is so altered
by books and lectures, by hearing and speaking, that the inward
can only speak to you through the outward, whatever you
pretend you can perceive.'

Mulakab: 'Does this apply to everyone?'

Simab: 'It applies to whom it applies. It applies above all to
those who think it does not apply to them!'

Displacement

A Sufi sheikh was asked why he did not accept the leadership of a group of disciples who wished to transfer their allegiance to him from their former leader.

He said:

'It is like the condition of a plant or another growing thing. To place oneself at the head of something which is dying is to partake oneself of the dying capacity of that thing. Individual parts can continue to flourish, especially if reinforced by something with greater truth. But the plant itself, when it has the power of death in it, will transfer that tendency of death to whatever connects with it as a whole.'

Someone asked him:

'But what was the situation in those historical instances when reformers and others have in fact taken over the headship of an activity, and it has gone on to greater strength?'

He said:

'Such were not teaching schools, but worldly activities which were only imagined by external observers and superficialists to be real entities.'

Dividing Camels

THERE was once a Sufi who wanted to make sure that his disciples would, after his death, find the right teacher of the Way for them.

He therefore, after the obligatory bequests laid down by law, left his disciples seventeen camels, with this order:

'You will divide the camels among the three of you in the following proportions: the oldest shall have half, the middle in age one-third, and the youngest shall have one-ninth.'

As soon as he was dead and the will was read, the disciples were at first amazed at such an inefficient disposition of their Master's assets. Some said, 'Let us own the camels communally,' others sought advice and then said, 'We have been told to make the nearest possible division,' others were told by a judge to sell the camels and divide the money; and yet others held that the will was null and void because its provisions could not be executed.

Then they fell to thinking that there might be some hidden wisdom in the Master's bequest, so they made inquiries as to who could solve insoluble problems.

Everyone they tried failed, until they arrived at the door of the son-in-law of the Prophet, Hazrat Ali. He said:

'This is your solution. I will add one camel to the number. Out of the eighteen camels you will give half—nine camels—to the oldest disciple. The second shall have a third of the total, which is six camels. The last disciple may have one-ninth, which is two camels. That makes seventeen. One—my camel— is left over to be returned to me.'

This was how the disciples found the teacher for them.

Revolting

'WHAT is your view about inner knowledge?' asked the mild-mannered dervish Abduh of the traditionalistic theologian Abdurrashid of Adana.

'I have no patience with it.'

'And what else?'

'It makes me sick!'

'And what else?'

'The idea is revolting!'

'How interesting,' said Abduh, 'that a logical and trained mind like yours, when asked for a view on a matter, can only describe, instead, three personal moods.'

Laws

THE Caliph Haroun el-Raschid was sitting in disguise one evening in a company of dervishes.

One of those present said:

'Rules can only function well with people for whom they were explicitly prepared.'

Haroun, who was dressed as a visiting merchant, objected:

'But surely this is a dangerous doctrine, for it would mean, if believed, that people could deny that laws applied to them.'

A Sufi ancient who was present said:

'Such a lack of understanding is, in reality, rare. If, on one of his secret nightly visits to various parts of this city, the Caliph heard of the belief in the limitation of laws, he might indeed be shallow enough to summon us to answer the following morning at his Court. Otherwise, it is not harmful.'

Example

ONCE upon a time there was a dervish whose reputation, due to his spiritual and temporal achievements, increased as the years passed.

One day he decided to marry. To the amazement of all who knew him, he chose the most evil-tempered woman for many miles around.

A certain wandering baba visiting him not long after his wedding could not restrain his curiosity at the sight of this saintly man constantly interrupted and criticized by a stupid woman.

He asked his host to explain the reason.

The dervish said:

'Brother, when you penetrate beyond the obvious, many things become clear. My wife's harangues, as it happens, prevent me from becoming too overbearing. Without her, my position as a sage might go to my head. Besides, there is always the chance that she may see, by contrasting her own conduct with mine, that she could modify her rudeness and ensure her own celestial bliss.'

'Imitation of the wise is indeed a thing to practise,' said the baba to himself. He was profoundly moved by the explanation and as soon as he arrived back at his own home, he married the foulest-tempered woman he could find.

She reviled him before his friends, relations and disciples. But his meekness only increased her scorn and derision.

Before many months had passed, the baba's wife had driven herself mad. She became so accustomed to bullying people without producing any reaction that one day she started an argument with an even more vicious woman—who killed her.

The widower baba took to the wandering life again, and

eventually found himself once more at the house of the dervish, to whom he recited his story.

The dervish said:

'If you had asked me, instead of rushing to practise a half-understood principle, I would have told you that it was not a general rule, and how to put it into operation in the individual case. In trying to do good to yourself, you have done evil to others.'

The Miracle

IMAM ALI, according to the *Durud-i-Qasimi*, admitted a barbarian stranger to his presence, in spite of the trepidation of those around him. Less than fifteen minutes had passed before the Imam said to his companions:

'This man will become a saint when he leaves this house, and his powers will seldom be excelled.'

Since Hadrat Ali had done no more than raise his right hand over the newcomer's head, his disciples asked one another why they could not receive a similar blessing, so that they could instantly be transformed in a like manner.

Ali said:

'This man had humility. As a consequence I was able to impart Baraka to him. Failure to exercise humility has made you difficult to act upon, because you are your own barrier. If you want proof of this arrogance, here it is: the humble man would assume that he could not learn without great effort and much time. Consequently he will learn easily and quickly. The arrogant imagine that they are ready, and agitate for the Baraka, refusing to entertain even the thought that they are unworthy. To be unworthy is one thing; to fail to realize that it is possible is another, and worse. Even worse is to imagine that one is humble or trying to be sincere when one is not. Worst of all is to think nothing until one sees someone—such as the barbarian stranger—to whom one feels so superior that one's actions become uncontrolled.'

Every Luxury

THERE was once a Sufi who was also a gifted business man, and he accumulated much wealth.

Another man, visiting him, was appalled by his obvious riches, and he said, 'I have just been to see such-and-such a Sufi. Do you know, he was surrounded by every luxury.'

When this was reported to the Sufi, he said:

'I knew that I was surrounded by almost every luxury; but not every single one. Now I know that on the day that man came, my collection of luxuries was complete.'

Someone asked him what the final luxury had been.

'The final luxury is to have someone to envy you.'

Unsitable

A KING who had amassed great wealth and many domains decided that he should become a dervish. He said:

'People universally respect these Sufi people, and it is not fitting that I, the king, should not partake of the merit which characterizes them.'

So he called a venerable dervish sage and asked to be enrolled in the Path of Wisdom.

The dervish said:

'With all respect and every regret, Your Majesty, you will never pass the test.'

The king said:

'Just try me, for it is possible that I might—after all, I have been successful in all my endeavours thus far in my life.'

The dervish said:

'Majesty, it would be improper for me to attempt a test which I know you will fail, for this is wasting effort and an absurdity. If, however, you agree to the examination taking place in open durbar, then I could agree, since your very failure might teach others present the problems of the Dervish Way.'

So the king agreed, and the court was convened.

'Let the examination proceed,' said the king.

'Very well,' said the dervish. 'I want you to answer "Yes, I believe you!" to every statement which I make.'

'That sounds easy enough,' said the king. 'Say on.'

The dervish then said:

'A thousand years ago I ascended into the heavens.'

'Yes, I believe you,' said the king.

'And as the generations passed, I did not age like other people,' said the dervish.

'Yes, I believe you,' said the king.

'I travelled to places where the rain fell upwards and the sun was cold and the people were smaller than the insects,' said the dervish.

'Yes, I believe you,' said the king.

'And', said the dervish, 'I managed to teach people who did not want to be taught, and I could not teach people who wanted to be taught, and when I was lying people thought I was telling the truth, and when I was saying only truth, they imagined that I was lying.'

'Yes, I believe you,' said the king.

'On one of my journeys, I came across your own parents, and they were liars, deceivers and paying a dreadful penalty for their crimes,' said the dervish.

'That is a lie!' shouted the king. 'I do not believe a word of it.'

Sayed Sultan

SAYED SULTAN said:

'If you pray, and feel satisfaction at having prayed, your action has made you worse. In such circumstances, cease to pray until you have learned how to be really humble.'

Three Men of Turkestan

THREE men of Turkestan were followers of a braggart ignoramus who spoke a few words of Persian. They called themselves his disciples; and he taught them three words. They each memorized one: 'We', 'were not' and 'happy'.

As soon as they had gained this knowledge, nothing could prevent them from starting off on their travels to visit a holy shrine, repository of all wisdom.

As soon as they entered Khorasan, however, they saw a dead man lying on the ground. They dismounted to look at this strange sight, and when they had done so, some Khorasanis came up and said:

'Who killed the man?'

'We,' said the first disciple, using the only Persian word he knew.

They were seized and taken to court. The judge said:

'Why were you standing around this body?'

The second disciple said:

'We were not.'

'That is a lie,' said the judge.

Then he asked:

'How do you feel if you kill a man?'

'Happy,' said the third disciple.

'These people must be monsters!' cried the Khorasanis.

The judge asked:

'What was the motive of the crime?'

The three cried out, using all their Persian:

'We were not happy!'

'They are undoubtedly incorrigible murderers,' said the judge, as he sentenced them to be hanged.

Feeling

Uwais was asked:

'How do you feel?'

He said:

'Like one who has risen in the morning and does not know whether he will be dead in the evening.'

The other man said:

'But this is the situation of all men.'

Uwais said:

'Yes. But how many of them *feel* it?'

The Precious Jewel

ALL wisdom, according to Daudzadah, is contained in the various levels of interpretation of this ancient traditional tale.

In a remote realm of perfection, there was a just monarch who had a wife and a wonderful son and daughter. They all lived together in happiness.

One day the father called his children before him and said:

'The time has come, as it does for all. You are to go down, an infinite distance, to another land. You shall seek and find and bring back a precious Jewel.'

The travellers were conducted in disguise to a strange land, whose inhabitants almost all lived a dark existence. Such was the effect of this place that the two lost touch with each other, wandering as if asleep.

From time to time they saw phantoms, similitudes of their country and of the Jewel, but such was their condition that these things only increased the depth of their reveries, which they now began to take as reality.

When news of his children's plight reached the king, he sent word by a trusted servant, a wise man:

'Remember your mission, awaken from your dream, and remain together.'

With this message they roused themselves, and with the help of their rescuing guide they dared the monstrous perils which surrounded the Jewel, and by its magic aid returned to their realm of light, there to remain in increased happiness for evermore.

The Price of a Symbol

WHEN he was asked, 'Why do you charge so much for your lessons?' Sayed Ghaus Ali Shah said, 'Why should I not?'

His questioner continued:

'Surely it did not cost you so much to gain your knowledge, or to live while imparting it?'

'On the contrary,' said the Sufi, 'it cost me so much that money is no equivalent for me, it is just a symbol to me, but it has relative reality to you.'

The Water-Wheel

IT is related that a man went to Hakim Omar Khayyam and said:

'My dearest wish is that you should accept me for your teaching, and confirm in me the truths which I have learnt from my earlier teachers, which have in fact led me to you.'

The Hakim took this man to a place where a water-wheel was running. He placed a piece of wood to join the wheel, and the water stopped running. Now he said:

'This piece of wood represents your earlier teachers. Wood may be placed in conjunction with a water-wheel to stop it temporarily—as, for instance, when a repair is needed.

'For the wheel, the thud when the wedge took effect might be a notable experience. It might acquire a taste for the state of stillness, with water running past it, in place of its own movement.

'Now the wheel, aware that the reverberation of the wood has ceased, may seek a similar experience. But can we accept that what the wheel needs is to receive another block of wood?

'Only the observer, dear companion, can see the whole of a picture. The picture itself may imagine anything. Imagination is not sight.'

Rauf Mazari

Few people who observed Rauf could understand why he sometimes seemed full of confidence, and sometimes unsure of himself.

Then someone noticed that he always acted and spoke in a less assured way, the lower the capacity or sincerity of the person who was visiting him.

Mazari said of this:

'I am so deeply disturbed by the inner state of people who are anxious that I reflect that state.'

Idlers often imagined that Rauf was of a nervous disposition. They were very confused when they found that his inner capacities were regarded as of the highest by the greatest Sufi sages of the age.

Meaning of a Legend

SAYED IMAM ALI SHAH draws attention to an ancient legend which uses the Egyptian pyramids as its framework, and then explains the way in which stories were devised for teaching purposes.

The story tells how a certain pharaoh had a secret chamber built in his pyramid-tomb during his lifetime, so that all his treasures could accompany him to the next world.

The builder, however, told his two sons, saying, 'I shall die poor, but you will be able to enter the treasury by this secret passage whose map I give you as your heritage, for the king is an usurper, and has accumulated the gold from poor people such as us.'

When the sons had taken away some of the gold, however, one of them was caught by a hidden trap. He persuaded his brother to cut off his head, so that the family would not be caught, and could continue to enter. After some argument, the brother did this, and made good his escape.

The king was surprised to find the body without a head. He gave orders for the body to be tied to a wall, and a watch kept on it. The relatives, he reasoned, would want the body back, and if they tried to reclaim it, he would have them captured.

But the surviving brother was clever. He got some skins of wine, loaded them on a donkey, and allowed them to spill on the road near the watching guards. The guards took some of the spoilt wine and drank it. When they were drunk the brother took the body away for burial.

The Sayed states that this tale illustrates that events are parallel with mental working. The treasure stands for accumulated human knowledge, the pharaoh is the delinquent tendency of the mind to prevent people learning something which is to their advantage. The father is the man who knows how to obtain the knowledge, and the two sons are two conditions of the human mind. The first brother represents the reckless yet imaginative function; the other stands for the surviving, active principle, which has as much inventiveness as the other.

'In this manner, as much as any other,' continues Imam Ali Shah, 'the service of humanity continues. Note well that the operation of the teaching takes place in an extraordinary manner.'

'It is not necessary for this story to be untrue for it to be significant for teaching illustration.'

Ardabili

ASKED why he never thanked anyone for doing anything,
Ardabili said:

'You may not be able to credit this, but if I thank them, they
will feel pleased, and that amounts to the same as if they had
been paid or recompensed for their trouble. If they are not
thanked, there is still a possibility that they will in future be
requited for their service—and such requital might be far
better for them. It might come, for instance, at a time when
they really need it.'

Inward and Outward Knowledge

THE orally transmitted teaching of Samarqandi includes this significant passage:

The outward scholar studies either for himself or because he wishes to be seen, heard or applauded.

The inner sage studies for the sake of knowledge, not for his own sake.

When the inner sage has attained his knowledge, he may become a worker or a teacher.

If he is a teacher, his only concern will be to entrust knowledge to those who can benefit from it in a real manner: not those who will try to use it to adorn themselves, to impress others, or to feel important.

Unfortunately, although the true inward scholar can easily understand which people want knowledge for unsuitable reasons, he cannot point them out directly to themselves, because their *nafs-i-ammara* (commanding-self, conditioning) denies its role so strenuously that it prevents real knowledge being gained if it can.

When real knowledge comes, the commanding-self is obliterated. Why should one wonder, therefore, that it fights so hard?

It is because of this that the Wise enjoin humility.

The Secret Teacher

A MAN found the secret teacher Khidr working as a ferryman.

Khidr read his thoughts, and said to him:

'If I approach people in the street and tell them what to do, they will think I am mad, or am doing it for myself, and they will not do it. If I dress like a learned or a rich man, and advise them, they will disobey or else simply try to please me, instead of trying to please that which I represent. But if I mix with the people and say a word here and a word there, some will listen, just as you yourself recognized me, and a thousand others did not.'

A Morning's Marketing

BAHAUDIN NAQSHBAND one morning went into the great market of Bokhara with a long pole. He started to shout hoarsely until a crowd gathered, amazed at such behaviour from a man of his fame and dignity.

When hundreds of people had assembled, uncertain of what to think or do, Bahaudin took up his pole and started to overturn stalls until he was surrounded by piles of fruit and vegetables.

The Emir of Bokhara sent a representative to Bahaudin's house, to ask him to attend court immediately, to explain himself.

Bahaudin said:

'Let the doctors of law be present, the chief courtiers, the senior administrators, commanders of the army and the most important merchants of this town.'

The Emir, together with his advisers, concluded that Bahaudin had gone mad. Deciding to humour him until they could have him committed to the Abode of Health, the Emir and his court summoned the people named by Bahaudin.

When all were assembled, Bahaudin entered the audience-hall.

'You are no doubt aware, Your Presence Bahaudin,' said the Emir, 'why you are here. And you know why the rest of us are here. Please therefore say anything which you have to say.'

Bahaudin replied:

'Sublime Gateway to Wisdom! It is known to all that a man's behaviour is always taken as an index of his value. This has reached such a stage with us that a man has to do no more to gain acclaim and approval than to *behave* in a certain manner, no matter what his inner state may be. Conversely, if a man merely *does* something considered objectionable, he is regarded as being objectionable.'

The king said, 'We do not yet understand what you are attempting to teach.'

Bahaudin said, 'Every day, every hour, in every man, there are thoughts and inadequacies which, if given vent to, would be illustrated by actions as damaging as my actions in the market-place. My teaching is that these thoughts and short-comings, due to insufficient understanding, *are* as damaging and retarding to the community and to the individual as if he were to behave in a riotous manner—and more so.'

'What', said the king, 'is the solution to this problem?'

'The solution', said Bahaudin, 'is to realize that people must be improved inwardly, not just prevented by custom from showing their coarseness and destructivity, and applauded if they do not.'

The entire court was so impressed by this remarkable teaching, says the chronicler, that a public holiday of three days was announced, to enable the people to celebrate the receiving of such wisdom.

Moss

A GROUP of Bahaudin's senior disciples who had been in Persia had arrived to sit at the feet of the Master. As soon as they were assembled, Bahaudin ordered them to listen to tales and recitations read by the most junior of the followers.

Someone expressed surprise. The Master said:

'If you follow yonder track half a day's march, you will come upon a beautiful, abandoned building. You will see that one side of the magnificent dome is covered with moss. If you enter it, you will find that some of the precious tiles have slipped, and lie on the floor. About the value and achievement of the building there is no doubt. But exposure to certain human and natural treatment has caused a loss of perfection.

'So it is with the senior disciples.'

Bahaudin and the Scholar

A FAMOUS scholar one day visited Bahaudin Naqshband.

All the disciples expected that the Murshid would engage him in discussion and refute his arguments, as he had done with all other scholastics for so many years.

When, however, the scholar was settled in Bahaudin's Court, the Murshid showed him every consideration, and matters of human thought and divine mysteries were never mentioned.

When the scholar had left, someone remarked, 'How unusual that a man of words should not try to engage the Maulana in debate. This is the first one whom we have seen here who could resist the temptation, even though they all know that their arguments are always overturned.'

This came to the ears of Bahaudin, who said:

'Nothing is strange when one knows the reason. This man who appears to be a scholar is a Sufi in disguise. He is an *abdal*. This word, which people generally take to mean "changed one" also means, as you will realize, "someone in disguise". That is what he is. Since he is a scholar to the world and a Sufi to Sufis, how could he come here and dispute in an academic manner? As to "temptation", only a scholar would be tempted to argue. A Sufi does not have the temptation, and so the question does not arise.'

Someone said, 'We should have thought of that! Next time we will know what to make of a silent scholar.'

Bahaudin said to his chief disciple, 'Answer him.' The chief disciple said, 'Alas, no! The next time a silent scholar will probably only be a stupid one intimidated by el-Shah's reputation ...'

Visiting and Obtaining

'THOSE who have visited us,' said Naqshband, 'and have not obtained what they really needed from that visit, have not really visited us. They will, moreover, never be sufficiently filled. From those who desire to talk to us, we have nothing to hear. To those who wish only to hear, we have nothing to say.

'Those who accept what they have received and do not imagine that they have received nothing, will be given much more. Those who want other than what they are offered here will be unable to receive anything, anywhere.

'Do you remember the man who was given gold when he wanted silver, and there was no silver to give him? He said, "I cannot spend this because it is not white." '

Bahaudin

SOMEONE said to Bahaudin Naqshband:

'You relate stories, but you do not tell us how to understand them.'

He said:

'How would you like it if the man from whom you bought fruit consumed it before your eyes, leaving you only the skin?'

Bahaudin Naqshband

THE people called scholars are appalled at two things: first they do not like the methods which we use to reach the ears of the people, because they think that what is to be communicated must be done either by intimidation or by complicated terminology. They are appalled at another thing: that we are said to be hostile to scholars.

But the reality is very different. The people who are called scholars are substitutes for scholars. There are few real scholars, and a superabundance of these other people. As a result, they have acquired the generic name for scholars. In countries where there are no horses, donkeys are called horses.

Storing and Transmitting

It is recorded that Sheikh Abu-Ali of Sind used to lecture to completely ignorant people, and meditated with groups of the deaf and dumb.

He said:

'If you can learn at all, it is only because present and former teachers have employed the method of imparting knowledge to intelligent people, to plants, animals, idiots and inanimate objects, as well as to self-satisfied disciples.

'Just as the water in the porous clay jar makes the jar wholesome and satisfied, and also slakes the thirst of the traveller, so too is our work concentrated and transmitted by what you would consider inert or unworthy vessels.'

How it Feels to be a Teacher

THE Nurbakshi writing on teachership has it:

'The teacher is like a master-craftsman in a country where people want craftwork but yet imagine that it is performed, shall we say, in the dark. He is like an eagle in a cage, deprived of his main capacity of flight and sight, but employed by idlers for visual amusement. He is like a lion in a pit, baited by the ignorant and admired by those who like a tawny coat. He is like the ant, who invented a house, and hopes that he can attain his object of inducing man to copy him. He is like the crow, showing man how to bury his dead, while man watches, perplexed, knowing that he can learn but not imagining what it is that he has to learn from what the crow is doing.

'All of the Wise have to learn how to pass on the knowledge. But they can do this only if the student will allow himself to learn what it is and how it is that he is to learn. Technique of learning is what the teacher has first of all to teach. Unless you are prepared to study the technique of learning, you are not a student. And if your teacher advises you to learn by words, or deeds, or by baking bread—that is your way.'

Founding of a School

A SUFI of the Order of the Masters was asked:

'Why did the Madmen of God, who traversed the earth in strange garb doing incomprehensible things, form schools for the transmission of the Teaching?'

He said:

'What they had to do, they did—and they still do. But as far as direct transmission from them is concerned, remember the passage:

When they were clear, there was nothing in what they said; when they were incoherent, nobody could benefit from what they said.

'This is the interpretation of the cryptic poem about our knowledge in the most ancient times—"If you could understand it, there was nothing there. If you could not, there was no profit, only imagination." '

Opulence

I⊤ is recorded that Haji Mohiyudin was studying under the ancient Master, Hallaj, when he was told:

'Leave my company, work until you have attained some wealth and position, saying nothing about your connection with us, and then return.'

The Haji was confused, and said:

'But I desire the path of renunciation, not the way of opulence.'

Hallaj answered:

'You are not ready for renunciation, and not proof against opulence. In addition, your remark shows that you wish to lay down your own path—how can you then benefit from a higher guidance?'

The Haji asked him:

'If I am setting down my own rules, and in obeying you only do so while it suits me, how can I be expected to deviate from this rigid behaviour and now take your orders in obedience, since you have characterized me as laying down my own path?'

Hallaj said:

'Initially, it is true, you will pretend to follow the path of opulence, and pretend to obey. But our hope is that this pretence will become repugnant to you.'

Wisdom

S<small>UFIAN</small> said:

'The wisdom which is invisible but which sustains is a hundred times better than the appearance of wisdom, for that has itself to be sustained.'

Luxury and Simplicity

THE Sufi ancient Junaid taught by demonstration, through a method in which he actually lived the part which he was trying to illustrate. This is an example:

Once he was found by a number of Seekers, sitting surrounded by every imaginable luxury.

These people left his presence and sought the house of a most austere and ascetic holy man, whose surroundings were so plain that he had nothing but a mat and a jug of water.

The spokesman of the Seekers said:

'Your simple manners and austere environment are much more to our liking than the garish and shocking excesses of Junaid, who seems to have turned his back upon the Path of Truth.'

The ascetic heaved a great sigh and started to weep.

'My dear friends, shallowly infected by the outward signs which beset man at every turn,' he said, 'know this, and cease to be unfortunates! The great Junaid is surrounded at this moment by luxury because he is impervious to luxury: and I am surrounded by simplicity because I am impervious to simplicity.'

The Caravan

An intending disciple said to Dhun-Nun the Egyptian:

'Above everything in this world I wish to enrol in the Path of Truth.'

Dhun-Nun told him:

'You can accompany our caravan only if you can first accept two things. One is that you will have to do things which you do not want to do. The other is that you will not be permitted to do things which you desire to do. It is "wanting" which stands between man and the Path of Truth.'

Giant Apples

A SUFI once visited a king, to advise him on matters of state, and the two became good friends. After some months the Sufi said, 'I must now move on, to work in private among the lowest people in your kingdom, in poverty and many miles from here.'

The king urged him to stay, but the Sufi assured him that he must do his duty.

'How shall I remain in contact with you?' asked the king.

The Sufi gave him a letter and said, 'If ever you receive incredible news about fruit from such-and-such a province, open this. Then my work will have been finished, and you will still have something to do.'

The Sufi journeyed to his destination, and lived like any ordinary individual there, carrying on his functions in accordance with the dervish science.

Some years later a certain man, thinking that the Sufi might have a hoard of money, killed him; but all he found was a packet marked 'giant apple seeds'.

He planted the seeds, and within an amazingly short time, apple trees bearing fruit as big as a man's head filled his garden.

People began to revere the murderer as a man of sanctity—for who else could stock his orchard in a matter of days, in mid-winter, with trees bearing fruit of such a size?

The murderer, however, was not content with this adulation. 'If I got no money from the man I killed,' he reflected, 'here is my chance now. I shall take them to the king, and he will certainly reward me.'

After many difficulties, he was shown into the presence of the monarch.

The murderer said, 'Your Majesty, I have in a basket here

an apple, the size of a man's head, which I have grown in a few days, in mid-winter, in such-and-such a province.'

At first the king was amazed at the sight of the fruit. Then he remembered the Sufi's letter. He called for it to be brought from the treasury where it had been kept, and opened it.

The letter said, 'The man who grows giant apples is my murderer, no matter what respect he has earned from it. Let justice now be done.'

Effort

ASKED about effort and prosperity, Zain el-Abidin said:

'The rich take refuge in prosperity, and make it their idol. The poor take refuge in poverty and make it their shackles.

'Only the Wise Ones know the real meaning and value of objects and efforts, and the circumstances and reason for opulence and show or the reverse.'

The New Initiate

ASHRAF ALI NIAZI was approached by a foreign visitor who said:

'I wish to become a Sufi and will do anything if I can be initiated; I have read such-and-such books, and met some Sufis in our own country.'

'This callow individual will assuredly have to remain here for years, if he is to learn even how to approach the Way—unless Hadrat Niazi casts him out immediately,' the disciples thought.

But the Sheikh at once said to the visitor:

'I shall initiate you at once. More, I shall make you my representative in your own country. Work on you own: I do not know the people whom you have mentioned.'

The disciples were almost all amazed.

When the visitor left, the Sheikh said:

'You have all imagined that I would cast him out or else give him tasks which would prepare him for enlightenment.

'You now imagine that I have done neither, but honoured him unnecessarily.

'But it is the reality, not the appearance, which functions.

'I have sent him away—that is a casting-out.

'I have told him that he is initiated and our representative. That is his exercise in preparing. If he imagines now that he should teach or enrol, and act as a representative, he will increase his own self-esteem and get nowhere. If he realizes that he is unsuitable for initiation and to be a representative, he will return, and I will then be able to instruct him.'

'But what about the people whom he might imagine that he is teaching, if he fails the test? Will he not harm them?' asked a disciple.

'Anyone who takes him for a teacher, or even an initiated Sufi,' said the Master, 'is already beyond our reach.'

Unanswerable

WHEN Jalaludin Rumi started to recite his couplets of wisdom, it is reported, people had not had enough time to form any opinion of him.

Some were interested, some were not. Others, following an inevitable human pattern, resented him. They said, 'We hope that you do not think that you are a second Æsop or something.'

Literalism

A WOULD-BE disciple presented himself to a Sufi in Baghdad, asking to be accepted for teaching.

'I will accept you as a probationer,' said the Sufi, 'and give you these first directions: that you do not consider yourself to have any belongings, and that you do not hold on to anyone else's property.'

The disciple agreed. Now the Sufi said, 'You must travel from here to Bokhara, living as best you can, and noting everything which happens. After that you should wait for further instructions from me.'

The disciple set off, and eventually reached Bokhara. He had only just arrived, however, when he felt a nip, and realized that he was host to a flea.

'This will never do,' said the disciple to himself, 'for I cannot remain in Bokhara as instructed when I have not fulfilled the whole of my first instructions. This flea, to be sure, I do not consider to be my own. But since it is assuredly someone else's property, I shall retrace my steps until I find its owner.'

Nobody would accept the flea until he arrived back in Baghdad, where it jumped off him—and he never saw it again.

Hilmi

THEY asked Hilmi:

'Why do you take so much interest in matters which are not connected with the progress of man?'

He said:

'When you want to know how hard the coppersmith has been working, you look at the shavings on his floor.'

The High Knowledge

ANIS was asked:

'What is Sufism?'

He said:

'Sufism is that which succeeds in bringing to man the High Knowledge.'

'But if I apply the traditional methods handed down by the Masters, is that not Sufism?'

'It is not Sufism if it does not perform its function for you. A cloak is no longer a cloak if it does not keep a man warm.'

'So Sufism does change?'

'People change and needs change. So what was Sufism once is Sufism no more.

'Sufism,' continued Anis, 'is the external face of internal knowledge, known as High Knowledge. The inner factor does not change. The whole work, therefore, is the High Knowledge, plus capacity, which produces method. What you are pleased to call Sufism is merely the record of past method.'

Charikari

CHARIKARI said:

'It is related that a grasshopper brought a blade of grass as his offering to King Solomon the Wise, son of David, on whom be peace.

'When a donkey wants to praise something, he says, "This is just like a thistle."

'When man wants to honour a wise man, he sets up a shrine for him and calls him a religious teacher.'

Hazrat Bahaudin Shah

BAHAUDIN was a mighty prince, active in administering the affairs of state, and unconcerned about things of the mind.

One day he decided that something must be done about the large number of rogues and vagabonds who had flocked to live in the shelter of his prosperous domain.

He instructed the guards that a month from that time all mendicants and wanderers were to be rounded up and brought into the courtyard of his castle for judgment.

A certain Sufi who was a member of Bahaudin's Court asked for leave at that time, and set off on a journey.

When the appointed day arrived, the vagabonds were collected and made to sit down in a huge group to await Bahaudin Shah.

Seeing so many evident undesirables seated before his fortress, Bahaudin Shah was extremely wroth. He harangued them at length, ending, 'The court decrees that you shall all be whipped as evil-doers and as a discredit to our domain.'

Then, in the midst of the prisoners, the Sufi courtier, dressed in rags, stood up and said:

'O Prince of the Family of the Prophet! If a member of your own court has been arrested because of his clothes, and has thereby been proved a rogue, we must take heed. If we are known to be undesirables only by our clothes, there is a danger that people might learn this custom—and start to judge rulers like yourself only by their clothes and not by their inner worth. What would then happen to the institution of just rulership?'

After this, Bahaudin abandoned his throne. He is buried near Kabul, in Afghanistan, where he is regarded as one of the greatest of all Sufi sheikhs. All dismount when passing his shrine, and the lesson has never been forgotten.

Difficult

A BAND of robbers came upon a sincere man who was trying to study the Way of the Sufis.

Finding that he had no possessions of any consequence, they began to whisper about what to do with him.

Suddenly he began to shout, 'No! No! Please give me time!'

The leader of the bandits said:

'Do not be so afraid—it is over in a moment. Since you might identify us in future, we are going to kill you. Death is really nothing, we have seen it many times!'

'Death?' said the man. 'I am not worrying about that. You were whispering and I thought you had decided to ask me to become really honest. That is what would have been difficult.'

This is the origin of the Sufi group called *Taifa-i-Duzdan* (the Band of Thieves) who were so impressed by this experience that they joined their victim.

Presents

A Sufi Master once announced that he was reviving the Ceremony of the Gifts in which, once a year, offerings were brought to the shrine of some celebrated teacher.

People of all ranks came from miles around to give their presents and to hear, if it were possible, something of the teaching of the Master.

The Sufi ordered the gifts to be placed in the middle of the floor of his audience-hall, with all the donors in a circle around them. He then stepped into the centre of the circle.

He picked up the gifts one by one. Those which had a name on them he returned to the giver. 'The rest', he said, 'are accepted.

'You have all come to receive a teaching, and here it is. You may now learn the difference between the lower conduct and the higher conduct.

'The lower conduct is what is taught to children, and it is an essential part of their preparation. It is to take pleasure in giving and receiving. But the higher conduct is to give without attaching, in words or thought, any obligation. Rise, therefore, to the second conduct, from the lesser to the greater.

'Whoever continues to take his refreshment from the lesser will not rise. You cannot receive payment in satisfaction on the lower level as well. That is the meaning of the teaching of restraint. Detach from lesser pleasures, such as thinking that you have done good, and realize greater attainment — that of really having done something useful.'

Nahas

THEY said to Nahas:

'Your predecessor, who has just died in this village, taught us so much, and we are grateful to him. We feel that we have been honoured by his presence. But he was here for thirty years, and we fear that if we have made only a little progress in the Science of Man in that time, we may all be dead before you have completed your mission with us.'

Nahas answered:

'You once hired a tiger to do your mousing. It is right to be grateful to him. But if you had had a cat, as it were, you would not have found it necessary to say what you have just said.'

Chances

'I VISITED a Sufi,' says Ibn Halim, 'and he gave a long discourse.

'There were many people there, for he attracted hearers from everywhere.

'Each discourse was a model of erudition.

'I said:

' "How do you have time to read so many books?' "

'He said:

' "I have time for what I do read."

'Then I realized that he had no books. I said to him:

' "How do you obtain all this information?"

'He said, admitting it, "By telepathy."

'I said:

' "Why do you conceal this from your disciples?"

'He said:

' "To make them concentrate on what is said, not on who is saying it, or how he acquired it."

'I said:

' "It seems that such disclosures spoil one's chances of knowledge. Then why do you tell me this?"

'He said:

' "Your chances were already spoilt before you came to me."

'I said:

' "Is there no hope for me?"

'He said:

' "Not while you try to induce Sufis to speak your jargon. If you use your jargon, you will become more and more dissatisfied, for you use the tongue of the dissatisfied."

'I said:

' "Does dissatisfaction not lead to a desire to change?"

'He said:

' "Too little dissatisfaction means no desire to change. Too much means no ability to change." '

Siyahposh

SIYAHPOSH was asked:

'Why do you not get to the heart of the matter, and give us arguments and proofs with which we can test our progress?'

He said:

'Sugar, flour, fat and heat are all very well separately. Combined, with time, they make delicious halwa.'

The Embassy from China

THE Chinese Emperor sent an embassy to Hakim Sanai, it is related.

Sanai at first declined to 'send his wisdom for the edification and study of the scholars'.

After much discussion, however, he agreed to submit some teachings. He also sent a secret letter, heavily sealed, to the Emperor. In it was the interpretation of the teachings.

The teachings consisted of twelve propositions, six walking-sticks, three embroidered caps and one engraved stone.

The Emperor submitted these objects to his scholars, giving them three years in which to investigate them and to report their findings to him.

At the appointed time, it was discovered that the scholars had written books on the subject, attacked one another, developed schisms and schools of interpretation, and used the objects for purposes ranging from decoration to veneration, from divination to instruments of corporal punishment.

The Emperor read the Hakim's letter. First it described all the developments which had occurred. Then it revealed the real use of the objects and propositions.

Finally it said, 'But because the information about the real meaning of these items has been delivered and not acquired, the audience is not ready for them and must, consequently, mis-apply them: communication plus agreement do not equal com-prehension.

'This letter, therefore, is the answer to the embassy's original question as to why I seemed reluctant to part with my secrets to the most learned men on earth. I was not reluctant — I was incapable.'

The Question

A RICH braggart once took a Sufi on a tour of his house.

He showed him room after room filled with valuable works of art, priceless carpets and heirlooms of every kind.

At the end he asked:

'What impressed you most of all?'

The Sufi answered:

'The fact that the earth is strong enough to support the weight of such a massive building.'

Transition

It is related that Shamsi Tabrizi plunged some books into water and took them out completely dry. Jalaludin Rumi is said to have been profoundly impressed by this feat, and to have accepted the teaching of Tabrizi as a consequence.

But Akib Haidar is reported to have received this information with incredulity. 'How,' he asked, 'could a man of Rumi's stature believe that what is obviously a conjuring trick might prove anything about the importance of Shamsi?'

Haidar preoccupied himself with this question for years. He decided to assume that Rumi would not have been deceived by a trick. He assumed further that Shamsi had indeed performed the deception. What remained to be found out was the meaning of the demonstration; for it was in this, Haidar believed, that a clue might be found to the secret language of the elect.

The Hujjat Ahil was the great chief of the Sufis of the age, and Haidar, when he found his way to him, asked the question which had been perplexing him for seventeen years.

Ahil, as soon as the question was put to him, said:

'Precisely, your assumptions are correct, but man is so obtuse that he can rarely see why such things are done. Tabrizi performed the trick in order to illustrate that there was a "transition" from the possible to the impossible, and back again. The trick is no more than an illustration, but it is highly instructional. If, for instance, you draw a picture of a cow walking into a barn for a countryman, you will be able to illustrate to him a hypothetical fact—that a cow can walk into a barn. If the countryman were to object that "this is not a cow, but rather a piece of paper" this would show his stupidity, because even a piece of paper can be used to indicate the possible. Similarly, the dry books showed the possible transcending of reality which man can attain.'

Seeing

IT is reported that Avicenna the philosopher said to a Sufi:

'What would there be to be seen if there were nobody present to see it?'

The Sufi answered:

'What could *not* be seen, if there were a seer present to see it?'

The Deputation from Syria

A SYRIAN deputation, composed of Jews, Christians and Muslim dervishes, together with others whose religion was not known, travelled by the perilous route through the Iraqs to Turkestan, where they attended the dargah (royal court) of Ahmed Yasavi, the Sufi Teacher of the Age.

They were met by the Master at the gates of the city and made welcome with valuable gifts and every sign of honour. In their guest apartments were furs and carpets, rareties large and small, and servants were assigned to wait upon them.

When the Thursday evening time for special exercises arrived, the guests were agog to be admitted to the Tekkia of the Master of Yasi.

But when the designated dervishes were called in from their work to enter the Tekkia, only four of the eighty-two pilgrims were allowed to go in.

Their chief sheikhs were wroth, and demanded to know the reason for this favouritism, saying to Yasavi's deputy:

'We were granted robes of honour by the Master, fed by him and entertained royally. How now can we be excluded from the moment for which we have waited all our lives?'

The deputy said:

'You did not feel discrimination in your favour when you accepted the gifts: you only feel it when you believe that you are being denied something. This is the behaviour of children.

'The Tekkia is the storehouse of the riches of the Other Worlds. It is children who insist upon all scampering into a shop full of sweets. Mature people, on the other hand, are content when their representatives have been admitted, to collect and bring back the portions for all of them.'

Literature

ꙮꙮꙮꙮꙮꙮꙮꙮꙮꙮꙮꙮꙮꙮꙮꙮꙮꙮꙮꙮꙮꙮꙮꙮꙮꙮꙮꙮꙮꙮꙮꙮꙮꙮꙮ

YAKOUB of Somnan, explaining the function of the literature which he used, said:

'Literature is the means by which things which have been taken out of the community, such as knowledge, can be returned.

'The similitude is as of a seed, which may be returned to the earth long after the plant from which it grew is dead, with perhaps no trace of it remaining.

'The learned may be millers of the grain-seed, but those whom we call the Wise are the cultivators of the crop.

'Take heed of this parable, for it contains the explanation of much irreconcilability of attitudes in the two classes of students.'

Environment

DEDICATION of an environment in which one works, as in the instance of a Tekkia where dervishes meet, carries its special rules and requirements.

The bootmaker will arrange his atmosphere and surroundings in such a way as to enable him to benefit most and to benefit his work.

The man of this world will arrange his house so as to gain and give pleasure. And the people of religion make their buildings such as to stir them inwardly.

The People of the Path, however, will employ such interior arenas as will correspond with who is to be practising there, and what the intention of the operation may be.

It is the height of folly to imagine that because one likes a certain room, it will contain the necessary atmosphere. It shows the division between the People of Rule and the People of the Path and of Truth, when the former like a place and the latter know what it is like; and when the former decorate a place and the latter avoid such things.

Only the Real Perceiver can judge whether the hearth has more Baraka than the palace; and which of the dervishes shall exercise in it.

To infringe this condition of operation is worse than putting a donkey in rosewater, for it causes the movement of the Law of Reverse Effect, when people who tamper with the celestial lose much more than they gain.

This is the statement of the Sheikh Abdallah el-Nuri of Khorasan.

Andaki

ANDAKI was asked:

'Understanding and kindness are a part of the Sufi Way—why should there be anything other than love and beauty—why should there be knowledge, for instance, and the passage of time, and such things as hesitation or reprimand?'

He said:

'A ripening peach needs sun and water. Have you not seen what happens when the beneficent sun shines too long or too strongly? It becomes a destructive curse. Water a plant correctly, and the water will be a true blessing for it. Water it too much, and the plant will surely rot and will suffer the pangs which will make it regard the water not as a blessing but as the instrument of its destruction.

'Give a man what he calls kindness continually, and you will sap him so that he becomes unhappy. Fail to reprimand when such a criticism can have an adequate effect for him, and you have erred. Refuse to countenance these things as possible, and you are not really asking the questions which you believed you posed.'

Buyer and Seller

I T is related by the dervish Salah Yunus that he was present when an argumentative would-be scholar was allowed to say the most crude and insensitive things to his teacher, Burhanudin.

Burhanudin said nothing, and when the man had left the lecture-hall, Yunus said to him:

'Will you not perhaps chastise that man, so that he may be able to see the desperate situation that he is in?'

Burhanudin said:

'We shall not see him again, for he had concluded that I am unable to answer his challenges, and he will therefore go elsewhere.'

'Is this', asked Yunus, 'the means which you employ to rid yourself of annoying people?'

'This is not the means,' said Burhanudin. 'This is the way in which I give the man what he wants. He wants someone with whom to differ and argue. I refuse to be that man, and this makes him seek another, even more anxiously. So he will go and find someone who relishes debate. In this way, as it were, we will have helped to bring the buyer and the seller together. If I cannot help this man to find what I have to give, I can at least help him to find what he really desires.'

Learning by Signs

EL HASHMA had the reputation of teaching by signs. A man who was greatly attracted by this idea travelled for years until he arrived at the sage's school.

As soon as he saw him, Hashma said:

'You must be prepared to learn, at least the first steps to wisdom, by words alone.'

The man protested:

'I can get words anywhere. I came to learn by signs.'

Hashma said:

'Everyone wants to learn by signs, gestures and exercises, since they have heard that it is possible. The result has been that they are too excited by the prospect to be able to do so. Such is their excitement that they cannot perceive it, and shout, "We are not excited!"

'Therefore we must resort to an alternative until they are ready — words and readings.'

The Pardoned Murderer

JAN FISHAN KHAN was asked about circumventing the opposition towards the Sufis, manifested without reason by so many people. He said:

'There was once a king who caught a man attempting to kill him. Since that king had taken an oath never to give orders for blood to be shed, he did not kill his attacker. Instead he devised a plan.

'He sent the man back to his own sovereign, with the message: "We have captured this man in the act of trying to take the life of the king. Having forgiven him, we send him back to you, complimenting you upon having at your disposal such a loyal servant."

'When this man arrived back at the court of his own monarch, he was instantly killed. He was not executed for failing in his mission, but because his master could not credit that anyone who attempted murder could have been forgiven and released unharmed. It was therefore concluded that he had bought his freedom by promising something — perhaps even to destroy his own king.'

Jan Fishan continued:

'When we are trying to teach man how to be balanced, we cannot accuse him of being unbalanced. His behaviour emphasizes the need for our work. If he were otherwise, we would have no function. Therefore human cruelty and destruction of what is vital to him is his everyday activity. He will be more likely than not to see the Sufis as bad, since he almost always acts against his own true interests.

'Has it not been said by the ancients, that "When man starts to understand the Sufi, there will be no more 'Sufis' and 'other men' "?'

Halabi

SULAIMAN HALABI always had a huge book lying on the floor, doing service as a door-stop.

An austere and opinionated visitor, unaware of Sulaiman's habits, bent as he entered, to pick up the book.

'Let it lie there,' said Halabi.

'Such disrespect towards any book is unworthy in the ranks of the Wise,' said the visitor.

'Even more unworthy', said Sulaiman, 'is it to imagine that a book which is useful for some people should be applied upon others, whether it suits them or not. It is worse than unworthy if one does not know that there are means of communicating knowledge which communicate knowledge, regardless of what they look like.'

The Abode of Truth

THERE were once two sages. One was deluded and many people believed that he was a great man.

The second sage was a true possessor of a higher knowledge. Many people, again, believed in him.

A natural catastrophe occurred, and both sages, together with their followers found themselves ranged before the Inquiring Angels who determine the future destination of human souls.

The Angels interrogated everyone. Then they announced that the followers of the first sage should go with him to Hell, and the community of the second sage were to accompany him to Paradise.

The two sages and the entire assembly of souls, however, were perplexed. They asked the Angels, 'On what basis is this decision made?'

The Angels said:

'Both sages and their people are believers. But the first sage, while imagining that he believed in something higher, in reality believed only in himself. His followers would not have been disciples of his had they not inwardly desired to worship him. The second sage believed only in Truth. His followers had been attached to him — and remained attached to him — only because inwardly they really sought not him but Truth.

'The afterlife is the Abode of Truth. If it were ruled by men, the story would be otherwise. But it is a reality, not a theory — so our decision is inevitable.'

Rights and Duties

A CERTAIN fakir saw a saddened dervish slowly walking away from the Tekkia of the great teacher Arif Hakimi of Paghman.

He asked the keeper of the gate what might the reason be for this man's crestfallen look.

The gateman replied, according to Ghalib Shah:

'He demanded the right to attend the meetings of the People of Truth. But the People cast him out, for those who have the right cannot demand it, and those who demand it cannot have it.

'As Abu-Yusuf himself was heard to remark:

' "The disciple does not need to speak a word before the Guide knows, through his demeanour and posture, whether he has come to learn or come to trade." '

Alisher Nawai

THEY asked Alisher Nawai why he did not write analyses of his poetry, so that people would know what to think of it, and how to study it.

He said:

'The miner brings the gem from the mine, and the engraver engraves it. The jeweller may sell it. If I were to do everything with these jewels, there would be no room for anyone else to profit.'

They asked him:

'So there should always be scholars to interpret? But that causes dissention, because scholars differ.'

He answered:

'There will always be goldsmiths, and they compete, vying with one another for fame and to sell their goods. Many fools will buy from fashionable goldsmiths. But there will always be real buyers, who can tell the good engraving. And they will have the money, never fear.'

The Design

A SUFI of the Order of the Naqshbandis was asked:

'Your Order's name means, literally, "The Designers". What do you design, and what use is it?'

He said:

'We do a great deal of designing, and it is most useful. Here is a parable of one such form.

'Unjustly imprisoned, a tinsmith was allowed to receive a rug woven by his wife. He prostrated himself upon the rug day after day to say his prayers, and after some time he said to his jailers:

' "I am poor and without hope, and you are wretchedly paid. But I am a tinsmith. Bring me tin and tools and I shall make small artefacts which you can sell in the market, and we will both benefit."

'The guards agreed to this, and presently the tinsmith and they were both making a profit, from which they bought food and comforts for themselves.

'Then, one day, when the guards went to the cell, the door was open, and he was gone.

'Many years later, when this man's innocence had been established, the man who had imprisoned him asked him how he had escaped, what magic he had used. He said:

' "It is a matter of design, and design within design. My wife is a weaver. She found the man who had made the locks of the cell door, and got the design from him. This she wove into the carpet, at the spot where my head touched in prayer five times a day. I am a metal-worker, and this design looked to me like the inside of a lock. I designed the plan of the artefacts to obtain the materials to make the key — and I escaped."

'That,' said the Naqshbandi Sufi, 'is one of the ways in which man may make his escape from the tyranny of his captivity.'

Ghazali
Practical Processes in Sufism

ALMOST a thousand years have passed since Ghazali wrote his monumental work *Restoration of Religious Sciences*. Much of it is applicable only to people and problems of the Middle Ages. But certain portions, summarized here, give vital basic information about the theory, structure, technical terms and means of proceeding in Sufism.

Ghazali shows that the element which the Sufis call 'knowledge' is employed as a technical term, and that its functions for the human being go far beyond what one would ordinarily regard as knowledge. More contemporary thinkers, and those writing with less danger of totalitarian counter-attack, would call this form of knowledge the very force which maintains humanity.

Knowledge, he says—the goal of the Sufi—is that which supports life to such an extent that if its transmission were to be interrupted for three days the kernel of the individual dies, just as someone would die if he were deprived of food, or a patient dies when deprived of certain medicines. Sufi knowledge, therefore, is something which continually pours into man. It is the perception and employment of this knowledge which is the aim of mystics. (Quoting Fatah el-Mosuli.)

Wisdom is sometimes used as 'understanding the special knowledge'. Sometimes this causes people to depart from ordinary habits. Naturally such conduct is opposed by the ordinary.

Ordinary people are those who are blind to the urgent need for knowledge. This blindness Ghazali likens to a disease. It causes arrogance. When there is arrogance, knowledge cannot operate.

The problem of men in seeking true knowledge is great because they do not know where to look for it or how to do so. This is because they have been deceived into mistaking rules and discipline, or scholasticism, or argument, for instance, as the search for knowledge.

What is this special knowledge which maintains man? It is so much more advanced a thing than, say, belief (what people call faith) that 'those who really know are seven hundred degrees in rank above those who only believe.'

Three traditional remarks about knowledge serve Ghazali as illustrations:

'Wisdom is so important that it might be said that mankind is composed solely of the Wise.' (Ibn el-Mubarak.)

'Whoever has knowledge and who works and teaches, he shall be mighty in the Kingdom of Heaven.' (Attributed to Jesus.)

'Solomon was offered wisdom, riches or power. He chose wisdom: and gained riches and power in addition.' (Ibn Abbas.)

Purpose of Following the Science of Knowledge

'The purpose of the exercise of the science of knowledge, or Sufism as it is known, is to gain an eternally durable existence. (Ghazali.)

' "Man" may die, but "wisdom" is immortal.' (Ali, son of Abu Talib.)

'All capacity not rooted in knowledge dies.' (Sakhr el-Ahnaf.)

Those Who Possess the Wisdom

'There are always wise people on earth. The Wise of the Age are the Luminaries of the Era. From the Illuminate of the Age the others receive their light.' (Al-Hasan.)

The Means

'Celestial knowledge comes about only through human effort.'

How the Science Is Pursued

'One is prayer, but the inner function of prayer must be understood. In prayer there is a secret significance. The exercises of prayer mark hidden elements.' (Ghazali.)

'One piece of knowledge learnt in the early hours is better than prostrating oneself in prayer a hundred times.' (The Prophet.)

The Stages of the Study

Ghazali arranged these stages, which have their counterparts in thought, action and inner exercises:

1. Silence
2. Audition
3. Remembering
4. Action
5. Transmission

It is the teacher who can guide his student as to the methods of following this curriculum.

From Whom One Learns

'The Seeker can learn only from the Wise. They and their students are partners in goodness. Compared to them the balance of mankind are savages devoid of virtue, because they are heedless of the most significant thing about their possibilities.' (Abu el-Darda.)

The Qualifications of the Seeker

'The requirement fixed for this knowledge is that the recipient can guard it without loss.' (Ikrima.)

The Urgency

'Search for knowledge while it is to be found. When those who have it die, it becomes concealed.' (Ibn Masud.)

'Gaining knowledge is equivalent to what is called "Fear of God" in conventionalized religion. Seeking it is the same as what ordinary people call "worship". Studying it is the same as praise. Striving for it is equal to holy warfare, effort. Teaching it is the equivalent of giving charity. Handing it over is rewarded.' (Ghazali.)

The Rules of the Schools

A LECTURE by Zulfikar:

The whole future of the well-being of the community of Truth depends upon the right thought and right studies of that community itself.

You may think that blatant opponents of Truth are its worst enemies. This is not so, because opponents may always see the errors of their thinking, while those who imagine that they are sincere members of the community of Truth will never find sincerity, since they are not seeking it: they think that they have it already.

The teacher may be stricter with his students than he can ever be with strangers, for the disciples need a higher form of Truth, they need intensive and energetic supervision. The strangers are not at the stage of being capable of working with a more intense form of Truth.

The similitude is as of the master teaching the finer points of grammar to students who already know the language. To give proper instruction, he has to be punctilious and make sure that every usage of the language is correct and every mistake pointed out.

If the master were not concerned, as when a casual or crude visitor shouts out in barbaric words, he will not trouble himself or anyone else by answering. It is always an affront to anyone to criticize him unless one has the status of being his teacher. When the master is teaching, let us say, the basic rules and vocabulary of the language, he is still on the level of relative crudity, and he will allow many mistakes to go unremarked, and will praise the successes. When the students have gone beyond the stage where they have need to be praised, when they are really serious enough to know how undesirable it is to have, say, bad pronunciation, they will adopt an attitude which will make them co-operate with the master in helping them make sure that they remember the finer points. To an outsider such intensity of effort may well look abnormal, but once the master and students are working together, the understanding is between them, and no outside individual can judge as to their relationship.

The relationship of a special kind can never be measured by the imaginings of another kind. And even the rules of the schools of shoemakers can never be the same as the rules of the schools of farmers.

Bahaudin Naqshband
Discipleship and Development

EXTRACTS from the Testimony of Bahaudin the Designer (Naqshband):

We are adjured constantly to study and make ourselves familiar with the lives, doings and sayings of the Wise because a link of understanding exists between these factors and the potentiality in ourselves.

But if, as have the literalists, we soak ourselves in these elements from motives of greed or marvelling at wonders, we will transform ourselves indeed; but the transformation will be animal into lesser animal, instead of animal into man.

The test which is placed in man's way is to separate the real Seekers from the imitation ones by this very method. If man has not addressed himself to this study through his simplest and most sincere self, he will be in peril. It is therefore better, did man but know it, to avoid all metaphysical entanglements rather than to allow himself to be acted upon by the supreme force which will amplify, magnify, his faults if he lacks the knowledge of how to cure the fault, or of how to approach the teaching so that his faults are not involved in the procedure.

It is for this reason that we say that there are many different spheres, levels, of experience of the truth.

The Wise have always concentrated upon making sure that their disciples understand that the first stage towards knowledge is to familiarize themselves with the outward, factual, appearance of that knowledge, so that, preventing it from rushing into the wrong area of their minds, it might await development when the possibilities exist.

This is the analogy of a man taking a pomegranate and keeping it until his stomach is in a condition to digest it correctly. If a man eats a pomegranate when there is something wrong with his stomach, it will make the ailment worse.

One manifestation of man's ailment is to want to eat the pomegranate at once. Should he do this, he will be in serious difficulties.

Now you have the explanation as to why the Wise continually supply materials to be stored in the heart, as grain is stored, with a view to the making of bread. Because this is experience and not grain, man in his crudity does not customarily feel able to understand this great truth and secret. The man to whom we speak is, therefore, a specially attuned sort of man — 'The Generous Miser' — that is, the man who can hoard when hoarding is indicated, and who will make available that which there is as and when it is able to exercise its optimum effect.

I was mystified for many months by my esteemed mentor's giving me things to speak, to think and do which did not seem to satisfy my craving for the spiritual life. He told me many times that the craving which I felt was not for spirituality at all, and that the materials which he was giving me were the nutritions which I needed. It was only when I was able to still my maniac desires that I was able to listen to him at all. At other times I said to myself, 'I have heard all this before, and it is highly doubtful', or else, 'This is no spiritual man', or, further, 'I want to experience, not to listen or to read.'

The wonderful thing was this, that my teacher continually reminded me that this was my state of mind, and although I was outwardly trusting him and serving him in everything, I was not able to trust him to the necessary extent, nor in the vital direction. Looking back, I realized later that I was willing at that time to yield far more far-reaching parts of my sovereignty than were needed; but I was not prepared to yield the minor ones which alone were the pathways to my understanding.

I refer to this because it is by rehearsal of the experience of others that people at a similar stage in the Path may be able to recognize their own state and profit by it.

I remember that I was always magnetized, transfixed by the dramatic, and became attentive whenever anything of great stimulation was said or done, but that the significant factors in my association with my teacher were the ones which I missed, sometimes almost entirely. Because of this, in spite of being continually employed in the work, I wasted as much as eight years of my life.

Then it must be remembered that there are the two kinds of everything. This is something which we normally do not imagine as existing, but it is fundamental. There is the keeping of company with a wise man and learning from him, in the right way, which is productive of human progress. Then there is the counterfeit, which is destructive. What makes us completely confused in this matter is that the feeling which accompanies the false discipleship or the ordinary keeping company, as well as its external manifestations in courtesy and seeming humility, is so able to make us imagine that we are religious or dedicated people that it is possible to say that this is due to what has been called the entry of a demonic, counterfeiting power, which persuades most of the very distinguished and compelling spiritually reputed people and also their followers, even down the generations, that they are dealing in spirituality. It even enables them to communicate this belief to those who are not of their number, so that their reputation gains credibility through the very people who misguidedly say, 'I do not follow his path, but I do not deny that he is a spiritual and a good man . . . '

The only corrective to this is the making use of the special-occasion timing by the Master who alone is able to say as to when and where and in what manner the exercises and other activities, even those which do not appear to have the smallest connection with spirituality, may be carried on. There is a confusion here because this is sometimes taken to mean that one must never read books or carry out processes without the direct supervision of the Master. But this common and shallow mistake is seen to be absurd when we realize that the Master may specify courses or reading or action for a number of people or for an individual, and that he may find it necessary from time to time for these to take what seems a conventional, indeed, a seemingly scholastic course. But what is vital here is not how things appear to the student, but that the Master has prescribed them and that he will intervene as and when there is a need for a change. All manifestations of opposition to this curriculum or any other disharmony with the Master are manifestations of the rawness of the pupil, and may not be taken into consideration by the Master or any of his intermediaries (deputies) since the student can either follow the course dutifully or he cannot. If he cannot, he ceases at that moment to be a student, and hence has no right even of comment. Only true students have the right of comment, and those who draw attention to themselves by questioning the course itself are not in the condition of being students at all.

Failure to observe this is common among scholastic emotionalists who have adopted Sufi procedures, because they do not realize that the curriculum is already erected on the basis of all the possible contingencies which include any and all feelings of the pupils. What is aimed at here is the operation of the teaching through the capacity. If he is disturbing the progress of the session or the work of the deputy, he is the opposite of a student, and this should be observed as a lesson by the company.

I am well aware that the principles are far from the accepted ones in the shallow world which is balanced on the basis of what people think of one another, including the problem which false teachers continually feel, which is the question of what other people think of them. But the central factor is whether the Teaching is operating, not whether people feel through their ordinary senses that they are being fulfilled.

In the latter case, you may be sure that nothing of real worth is happening at all.

This is the end of the first section of the Testimony of Bahaudin Naqshband, the Designer.

Counsels of Bahaudin

YOU want to be filled. But something which is full has first to be emptied. Empty yourself so that you will fill properly, by observing these counsels, which you can do as duties to yourself:

FIRST

Never follow any impulse to teach, however strong it might be. The command to teach is not felt as an impulsion.

SECOND

Never rely upon what you believe to be inner experiences because it is only when you get beyond them that you will reach knowledge. They are there to deceive you.

THIRD

Never travel in search of knowledge unless you are sent. The desire to travel for learning is a test, not a command.

FOURTH

Never trust a belief that a man or a community is the supreme one, because this feeling is a conviction, not a fact. You must progress beyond conviction, to fact.

FIFTH

Never allow yourself to be hurt by what you imagine to be criticism by a teacher, nor allow yourself to remain elated because of praise. These feelings are barriers in your way, not conductors of it.

SIXTH

Never imitate or follow a man of humility who is also mean in material things, for such a man is being proud in material things. If you are mean, practise generosity as a corrective, not as a virtue.

SEVENTH

Be prepared to realize that all beliefs which were due to your surroundings were minor ones, even though they were once of much use to you. They may become useless and, indeed, pitfalls.

EIGHTH

Be prepared to find that certain beliefs are correct, but that their meaning and interpretation may vary in accordance with your stage of journey, making them seem contradictory to those who are not on the Path.

NINTH

Remember that perception and illumination will not at first be of such a character that you can say of them 'This is perception' or 'This is illumination.'

TENTH

Never allow yourself to measure everything by means of the same time measurement. One thing must come before another.

ELEVENTH

If you think too much of the man, you will think in a disproportionate manner about the activity. If you think too much about yourself, you will think wrongly about the man. If you think too much about the books, you will not be thinking correctly about other things. Use one as a corrective for the others.

TWELFTH

Do not rely upon your own opinion when you think you need books and not exercises. Rely less upon your belief when you think you need exercises and not books.

THIRTEENTH

When you regard yourself as a disciple, remember that this is a stage which you take up in order to discover what your true distance is from your teacher. It is not a stage which you can measure, like how far you stand from a building.

FOURTEENTH

When you feel least interested in following the Way which you have entered, this may be the time when it is most appropriate for you. If you imagine that you should not go on, it is not because you are not convinced or have doubts. It is because you are failing the test. You will always have doubts, but only discover them at a useful time for your weakness to point them out.

FIFTEENTH

Banish doubt you cannot. Doubt goes when doubt and belief as you have been taught them go. If you forsake a path, it is because you were hoping for conviction from it. You seek conviction, not self-knowledge.

SIXTEENTH

Do not dwell upon whether you will put yourself into the hands of a teacher. You are always in his hands. It is a question of whether he can help you to help yourself, for you have too little means to do so. Debating whether one trusts or not is a sign that one does not want to trust at all, and therefore is still incapable of it. Believing that one can trust is a false belief. If you wonder, 'Can I trust?' you are really wondering, 'Can I develop a strong enough opinion to please me?'

SEVENTEENTH

Never mistake training for ability. If you cannot help being what people call 'good' or 'abstemious', you are like the sharpened reed which cannot help writing if it is pushed.

EIGHTEENTH

When you have observed or felt emotion, correct this by remembering that emotions are felt just as strongly by people with completely different beliefs. If you imagine that this experience — emotion — is therefore noble or sublime, why do you not believe that stomach-ache is an elevated state?

NINETEENTH

If a teacher encourages you, he is not trying to attach you to him. He is trying, rather, to show you how easily you can be attracted. If he discourages you, the lesson is that you are at the mercy of discouragement.

TWENTIETH

Understanding and knowledge are completely different sensations in the realm of Truth than they are in the realm of society. Anything which you understand in an ordinary manner about the Path is not understanding within the Path, but exterior assumption about the Path, common among unconscious imitators.

The Legend of Nasrudin

A CERTAIN crafty villain was entrusted with the education of a number of orphans. Observing that children have certain strengths and weaknesses, he decided to take advantage of this knowledge. Instead of teaching them how to acquire a skill in learning, he told them that they already possessed it. Then he insisted upon their doing some things and refraining from others, and thus kept most of them blindly subject to his direction. He never revealed that his original commission had been to teach them to teach themselves.

When these children grew up, he noticed that some had detached themselves from his authority, despite all his efforts, while others remained bound to it.

He was then entrusted with a second school of orphans. From these he did not directly demand obedience and respect. Instead, he enslaved them to his will by telling them that mental culture was the sole aim of education and by appealing to their self-pride. 'The mind', he told them, 'will give you universal understanding.'

'This must be true,' thought the children. 'After all, why should we not be able to solve all problems by ourselves?'

He supported the doctrine by demonstrations. 'This man', he said, 'is enslaved by his emotions. What a disastrous case! Only the intellect can control the emotions. That other man, however, is ruled by his intellect. How much happier he is, how free from emotional frenzy!'

He never let the children guess that there was an alternative to the choice between emotions and intellect, namely intuition which could, however, be overcome or blurred by either of these, and always dismissed its appearance as irrelevant coincidence or guesswork. There are two kinds of 'habit': one derived from mere repetition, the other from intuition harnessed both to the emotions and to the intellect. But since intuitive habit is associated with true reality, this villainous old man simply abolished it in favour of repetitive habit.

Some of the children, nevertheless, suspected that certain miraculous aspects of life did not fit into his fragmentary pattern, and asked him whether there was not, perhaps, something else undisclosed, some secret power. He told one group of questioners, 'Certainly not! Such a notion is superstitious, and due to faulty mental processes. Do not put any value on coincidence. "Coincidence" means no more than accident, which though perhaps of emotional interest, lacks all intellectual significance.'

To another group he said, 'Yes, there is more in life than you will ever know; because it cannot be acquired by honest extension of the scientific information which I gave you, or which you manage to collect under my direction.'

But he took care that the two groups did not compare notes and so realize that he had given two contradictory answers. Now, from time to time, when the children reported inexplicable events to him, he consigned these to oblivion as having no scientific relevance.

He knew that, without taking stock of intuition, the children would never escape from the invisible net in which he had bound them, and that the intuitive knowledge of secrets excluded from their education could be won only when they were in a certain harmony of mind with the emotions. So he taught them to ignore variations in their mental condition; for once they discovered that powers of apprehension vary from hour to hour, they might guess how much he had concealed from them. His training confused their memory of such intuitions as they had been granted and they were willing to think along the logical lines he had prepared for them.

The children whom this villain had mistaught in his first school were now grown up, and since he had let them come nearer to understanding the true nature of life, certain casual remarks that they made to members of the second school disturbed their faith in scientific truth. So he hastily gathered those of the first school who still remained loyal to him and sent them out to preach incomprehensible doctrines purporting to explain the hidden mechanism of life. Then he directed the attention of the second school to these teachers, saying, 'Listen carefully, but never fail to use your intellect.'

The intellectual children soon found that there was nothing to be learned from these doctrines and said, 'They contradict logic. Only with logic are we on firm ground.'

Yet some members of the first school who had broken away from the old villain's teaching reproached them, saying, 'We, too, reject these doctrines, but that they fail to explain the secret mechanism of life of which you are in search does not deny its existence.' They answered, 'Can you, then, put the secret in logical terms?' but were told that to do so would be to deny its truth.

So they protested, 'Nothing is true that cannot face the cold light of reason.' A few, however, cried out, 'We are ready to believe everything you tell us. We think you are wonderful.' But they were as hopelessly lost as the intellectual children and the teachers of the incomprehensible doctrine, because they trusted only to a slavish credulity, not to the habit of intuition.

A state of educative chaos supervened. So many different ways of thought were current that it was often said, 'I cannot trust anyone. I must find out for myself by the exercise of my supreme will.'

The old villain who had bred this confusion thrived on it like a madman rejoicing in deeds of violence. Especially his cult of the intellect encouraged egotism and discord. And to those who still felt an inner uncertainty, a sense of incompleteness, or a hankering for something whole and true, he said, 'Distract your minds by ambition!' He taught them to covet honours, money, possessions, sexual conquests, to compete with their neighbours, to immerse themselves in hobbies and diversions.

It is said that when a horse cannot find grass, it will accepts

193

hay. For want of the green grass of Truth they accepted the dry hay with which he filled their mangers.

The old man devised more and more distractions for them: vogues, crazes, lotteries, fashions in art, music and literature, sporting competitions and all kinds of achievements which offered them temporary relief from this sense of lack. They were like a patient who accepts palliatives from his physician because he assures them that his disease is incurable. Or they were like the monkey and the crab-apple: he clutched the crab-apple inside a bottle, but the neck was too narrow for him to withdraw his hand and the crab-apple too. Unable to escape because hampered by the bottle. he was soon captured and put into a sack. But he proudly cried, 'I still have the apple.'

The fragmentary view of life forced on mankind by the old villain was now accepted; and the few people who tried to point out where Truth really lay were thought insane and readily refuted by the old argument, 'If what you say is true, then prove it to us logically!'

False coin is accepted only because true coin exists, and deep in their hearts many people knew this. But they were like children born in a house from which they had never been allowed to stray, doomed to walk from one room to another without knowing that there could be another house, elsewhere, with different furnishings and a different view from its windows.

Nevertheless the tradition that true coins exist, that there is another house, and that some horses eat grass, not hay, survived in a book which was not a book, delivered by direct succession from an ancient sage to one of his descendants named Hussein. Hussein searched the world until he found the man who through craft and guile would give the teaching of this book fit expression: namely, the incomparable Mulla Nasrudin. Thereupon this book which was not a book was interpreted by the actions of a Mulla who was no Mulla; who was both wise and a fool; who was both a man and many men. And the teaching was thus brought to the attention of the children who had been misled.

194

Mulla Nasrudin broke out of the net which had been cast by the old villain. For how can one burn a book which is not a book? How can one name a fool who is no fool? How can one punish a man who is a multitude? How can one strike a man who is oneself?

Study the adventures of Mulla Nasrudin, plumb the depth of the subtleties! He is like a tree which has nourishment in its roots and an edible sap; whose leaves are pot-herbs, whose flowers, fruit, branches and seeds are all variously the same!

Can a tree be a man, or a man a tree?

The Sufi Quest

by Ustad Hilmi, Mevlevi

MAN, we say we know, originates from far away; so far, indeed, that in speaking of his origin, such phrases as 'beyond the
stars' are frequently employed. Man is estranged from his
origins. Some of his feelings (but not all of them) are slight in-
dicators of this. This is why we speak of 'separation from the
beloved'; but these are technical terms, and those who employ
them to increase their emotional life are — increasing their
emotional life.

Man has the opportunity of returning to his origin. He has
forgotten this. He is, in fact, 'asleep' to the reality.

Sufism is designed as the means to help awaken man to the
realization, not just the opinion, of the above statements. Those
who waken are able to return, to start 'the journey' while also
living this present life in all its fullness. Traditions about
monasticism and isolation are reflections of short-term processes of training or development, monstrously misunderstood
and grotesquely elaborated to provide refuges for those who
want to stay asleep.

However improbable all this seems, it happens to be true.
It is, of course, no less probable than many other things believed by man. Some such beliefs are certainly erroneous: we
all know individuals with beliefs which we are convinced *are*
erroneous. On the other hand, since Sufism depends upon
effectiveness, not belief, Sufis are not concerned with incul-
cating and maintaining belief. 'I believe this is true' is no sub-
stitute for 'This is how it is done.' The two things are in reality,
if not in appearance, poles apart.

If man finds himself again, he will be able to increase
his existence infinitely. If he does not, he may dwindle to

vanishing-point. Those who see a threat or promise in such a statement are unsuitable for this work. There is no threat or promise in facts: only in the interpretation man makes of them.

People have been sent, from time to time, to try to serve man and save him from the 'blindness' and 'sleep' (which today would be better described as 'amnesia') which is always described in our technical literature as a local disease. These people are always in touch with the Origin, and they bring the 'medicine' which is half the cure. The other half, as in orthodox terrestial medicine, is the activity of that which is acted upon, to attain its own regeneration with the minimum of aid. These cosmic doctors — a literal translation of a most ancient term — often live in the world almost unnoticed, like the camel in the desert. They have been of all races, and they have belonged to all faiths.

Essentially, religion has two roles, which in all surviving systems have become confused through the absence of specialist knowledge in the publicists and most visible and active theoreticians. The first is to organize man in a safe, just and peaceful manner, to establish and help maintain communities. The second is the inward aspect, which leads people from the outward stabilization to the performance which awakens them and helps to make them permanent.

Numerous residual systems for human progress continue to float around in the world, but virtually all are devoid of value in this inner aspect, though they may not be without historical interest. Certainly they can show us at a glance that they are only employed for personal and community sentimental satisfactions — whatever their own imaginings about the matter may be. They can most charitably be described as vehicles abandoned by their builders and now occupied by half-comprehending amateurs who seek only a relief from thought about their predicament.

'The Teaching', however, operated by those whom we call 'The Wise', continues and may take any form. It is preserved intact and constantly nurtured by certain Sufis. Well-meaning but imitative groupings based on Sufism, and of no value to this inner side of 'the Work' exist side by side with real ones.

Recognizing a 'True Master' is possible only when the postulant, man or woman, is what we call 'sincere'. This technical term refers to his condition, not his opinions. Sincere means that he is objective enough to recognize the specialist and the nature of the task. To reach this stage, the Seeker has to learn to set aside, at least for a time, superficial assessment about the teachers, the Teaching and himself. By superficial we mean something quite precise: automatic assumptions based upon rules employed in testing a different type of phenomenon.

A person may be attracted to Sufism because of the wrong motives—such as curiosity, desire for power, fear, insecurity—but in spite of this he has a chance to develop understanding of the work. If, however, he merely deepens his attachment and increases his acquisitiveness, he is not a Sufi, and is most unlikely to become one. He is taking and consuming smaller stimuli than he need, though perhaps unable to prevent himself from craving such stimuli.

Sufism has two main technical objectives: (1) to show the man himself as he really is; and (2) to help him develop his real, inner self, his permanent part.

Though man 'originates from far away, is asleep and may return after he has attained the means' he can do so only if he works from a sound environmental base in the world in which we find him: our slogan is 'Be *in* the World, but not *of* the World.'

The Sufis, it is admitted on all sides by externalist students, have produced some of the world's greatest literature, particularly in tales, illustrative recitals and poetry. Unlike professional literary workers, however, they see this as a means to work, not an end of their work:

'When the Higher Man does something worthy of admiration, it is an evidence of his Mastership, not the object of it.'